From the Author of *Dog as My Doctor,*

MW00488394

Paws for the Good Stuff

A dog lover's journal

for creating a happier & more *pawsitive* life!

By Carlyn Montes De Oca

Illustration & Design by Giulia Notari

GOOSE HILL PRESS

Paws for the Good Stuff
Copyright © 2018 by Carlyn Montes De Oca
All rights reserved

No part of this publication may be reproduced, distributed, or transmitted in any form or by any means including photocopying, recording, digital scanning, or other electronic or mechanical methods, without the prior written permission of Goose Hill Press except in the case of brief quotations embodied in critical reviews and certain other noncommercial uses permitted by copyright law. For permission requests, please contact Publisher@GooseHillPress.com.

First Edition Published 2018

Printed in the United States of America

Print ISBN: 978-0-9997812-0-3

Library of Congress Control Number: 2018905367

Illustration & design by Giulia Notari

For special orders, bulk purchases, sales promotions, corporate sales, fund-raising and more contact Publisher@GooseHillPress.com.

This book is not intended as a substitute for the medical advice of physicians or veterinarians. The reader should regularly consult a physician in matters relating to his or her health and a veterinarian regarding their companion's health, particularly with respect to symptoms that may require diagnosis or medical attention.

To all who love and cherish their dogs...
You are stronger than you know.
May you find the courage to live pawsitively.

This Journal Belongs to

_____

and to

_____

friends forever

Me & My Best Friend

Add a selfie of you with your dog in the frame above.
Don't have one? Then get creative and doodle one.
Have fun! This is your *pawsitive* journal after all.

Paws·i·tiv·i·ty

an optimistic attitude
inspired by animals

Contents

"

My fashion philosophy is: if you aren't covered in dog hair, your life is empty.

ELAYNE BOOSLER

Why Paws for the Good Stuff?

Think of the last time you felt truly happy...

Were you smiling? Did you feel on top of the world? What did you dare to dream?

Having a *pawsitive* outlook helps you see life's challenges differently. When I'm laughing, the world feels brighter. When I'm smiling, others smile with me. When I'm optimistic, that energy is contagious.

We can't be happy 100% of the time. And that's OK. Sadness, grief, anger — these emotions are a natural part of the human condition. The problem is when we allow our negative feelings to linger, become chronic, and negatively affect our quality of life. When this happens not only do we suffer but those around us also feel our negative energy. When we become captive to this downward spiral, happiness feels forever out of our reach.

Gratitude → Pawsitivity → Happiness

I am not naturally optimistic. My smiles come from a choice I made many years ago to be happier by choosing a *pawsitive* mindset that I work on every day. Over the years, as I've surrounded myself with rescue animals (most of them dogs), I've discovered that when I tune into my animal friends, open my heart to their ageless wisdom, and express my gratitude for all they are and all they teach me; this is when my mindset shifts for the better.

Our canine BFFS model admirable qualities like playfulness, loyalty, grace, gratitude, courage, enthusiasm, and unconditional love; *pawsitive* qualities that we humans can greatly benefit from. When we start becoming aware that our animal friends are more than just pets — and are instead nature's delightful teachers, life's wise masters, and sages of simplicity — we open the door to the *pawsitive*, to greater happiness, and ultimately to our own transformation.

I created *Paws for the Good Stuff* as a companion to my award-winning book, *Dog as My Doctor, Cat as My Nurse,* because I noticed that the one thing many of my clients were omitting when it came to their well-being was a gratitude practice. Starting your day with a healthy breakfast is excellent, but gratitude is the breakfast of champions for the mind and spirit.

I also made this journal for myself because I want to uncover, nurture, and feel happier; I want to become more resilient in these ever challenging times; and I want to live a life of greater connection with my animal friends. In *Paws for the Good Stuff,* I believe these roads intersect. I would love for as many dog lovers as possible to join me on this marvelous journey of exploration and empowerment. Happier people create a more hopeful world and boy do we need that now more than ever.

We can all use a helping hand from time to time, but for those of us who feel that happiness is where our dogs are, it's a loving paw that can break our hearts open and transform our lives.

Stay *Pawsitive!*

Discoveries & Benefits

The Power of Your Subconscious

Your subconscious mind is most active during two times of the day: when you first wake up in the morning and when you are drifting to sleep. These receptive states are the best moments to give your brain and body time to pause, take note, and discover how your canine BFF can inspire you to be *pawsitive*.

Inside This Journal You Will Discover...

- 🐾 6 months (24 weeks) of journal pages *plus 2 bonus weeks*

- 🐾 Weekly Challenges every 7 days

- 🐾 Monthly Milestones every 28 days

- 🐾 Fun illustrations

- 🐾 Canine fun facts

- 🐾 Daily inspiring quotes

- 🐾 A secret link to 6 short videos where I share exclusive tips, helpful resources, and useful suggestions

- 🐾 *Dig Deeper* prompts to enhance, enrich, and enliven your journaling adventure

Discoveries & Benefits

Benefits of *Paws for the Good Stuff*

- 🐾 Sets you up for a more joyful day

- 🐾 Promotes mental & emotional well-being

- 🐾 Increases mindfulness

- 🐾 Helps replace negative thoughts with a *pawsitive* mindset

- 🐾 Boosts your emotional intelligence

- 🐾 Allows you to connect with your dog in a new and more meaningful way

- 🐾 Reflecting on your *pawsitive* day can help you get a better night's sleep

- 🐾 Creates a one-of-a-kind keepsake of lasting memories with your beloved dog

- 🐾 Reminds you that **you are 'the good stuff!'**

But, But, But, And...

But *I feel resistant to doing this.*
And you are not alone. Humans are resistant to change. Yet change is how we grow, discover who we are, and what we are capable of becoming. This journal will help you get out of your head and move into your heart; the number one place our dogs prefer to live.

But *I don't have time.*
And if you don't have 5 minutes to give yourself in the morning and at night, then you are absolutely right — this journal is not for you. If you want to feel happier, more *pawsitive*, and to take your life to the next level, then give yourself the gift of at least 5 minutes of quality time every single day and night.

But *I've done journals before and they haven't worked for me.*
And we've all tried things that haven't worked, but *Paws for the Good Stuff* is a unique journal for dog lovers. No other exists quite like it. What would you lose by trying a new approach based upon your connection, friendship, and love for your canine friend? If you learn one thing about yourself through this journey, if you feel even a little bit happier, a tad more *pawsitive* — won't it be worth it?

Pawsitive Tips

Let go of being perfect and
embrace yourself, just as you are.

Commit to your daily journal.

Smile often, laugh a lot,
and stay *pawsitive!*

How to Use Your Journal

Keep *Paws for the Good Stuff* and your favorite writing instrument on the nightstand next to your bed. In the morning, as soon as you wake up, take three deep breaths to get yourself ready.

Open your journal and take a few minutes to answer the three short questions in the AM section.

At bedtime answer the questions in the PM section. As you drift off to sleep, do the last prompt in your mind (and your heart) for 1 – 2 minutes before zzzzzzz...

Pawsitive Power Words

Each day you will be asked to choose a *Pawsitive* Power Word to use throughout your day. If you have trouble coming up with one on your own, borrow one of ours!

brilliant cheerful oneness family
connection grace forgiveness
love hope
empowered beautiful compassion
wisdom appreciation fun
playful terrific magic
courage whole-hearted
gratitude joyful stillness

Sample Page

A positive attitude causes a chain reaction of positive thoughts, events and outcomes. It is a catalyst and it sparks extraordinary results.

WADE BOGGS

Date _____ **May 22**

Pawsitive Power Word _____ **Joy**

am

This morning I woke up feeling _____ **grumpy** _____ and I'd prefer to feel _____ **happy.**

I am grateful to my dog because _____ **he is always there when I need him.**

How can my BFF inspire me to have a more *pawsitive* day?

No matter what kind of day I've had at work, Rudy is always so happy to see me when I come home. I feel so appreciated by him. Today, maybe I can appreciate someone else a little bit more.

pm

3 *pawsitive* things that happened to me today were...

- 🐾 **I made a new friend at work.**
- 🐾 **I found a penny on the ground and made a wish.**
- 🐾 **I told my co-worker Jackie how much I appreciated her and she gave me a hug!**

Tonight as I drift off to sleep I will send happiness & *pawsitive* thoughts to...

Jackie.

Sample Page

Before you get a dog, you can't quite imagine what living with one might be like; afterward, you can't imagine living any other way.

CAROLINE KNAPP

Date _____ **May 23** _____

Pawsitive Power Word _____ **Discovery** _____

am

This morning I woke up feeling **tired** and I'd prefer to feel **more energized.**

I am grateful to my dog because **She always wants to play and makes me laugh.**

How can my BFF inspire me to have a more *pawsitive* day?

I'm going to make an effort to laugh more... or at least smile.

pm

3 *pawsitive* things that happened to me today were...

- **I dropped my bag on the sidewalk and a nice woman helped me pick up my things.**
- **I watched a hummingbird outside my window as I ate my lunch.**
- **A little kid smiled at me. That made my day!**

Tonight as I drift off to sleep I will send happiness & *pawsitive* thoughts to...

That little kid.

My Pawsitive Commitment

I, _____

commit to a *pawsitive* life by writing in this journal every
morning and every evening for **at least the next 30 days.**

I will embark on my *pawsitive* journey
with focus, an open mind, and a sense of fun!

At the end of every 30 days I'll celebrate by reminding
myself how amazing I am. Of course, I will also make sure to let
my dog know that she/he is pretty darn sensational too!

_____

Today's Date

_____

Your Signature

_____

Witnessed By

_____

And now...

Paws for the Good Stuff!

*No pessimist ever discovered the secret of the stars, or sailed
to an uncharted land, or opened a new doorway for the human spirit.*

HELEN KELLER

Date _____

Pawsitive Power Word _____

am

This morning I woke up feeling _____ and I'd prefer to feel _____

I am grateful to my dog because _____

How can my BFF inspire me to have a more *pawsitive* day?

_____

_____

pm

3 *pawsitive* things that happened to me today were...

🐾 _____

🐾 _____

🐾 _____

Tonight as I drift off to sleep I will send happiness & *pawsitive* thoughts to...

_____

Dogs do speak, but only to those who know how to listen.

ORHAN PAMUK

Date _____

Pawsitive Power Word _____

am

This morning I woke up feeling _____ and I'd prefer to feel _____

I am grateful to my dog because _____

How can my BFF inspire me to have a more *pawsitive* day?

_____

_____

pm

3 *pawsitive* things that happened to me today were...

🐾 _____

🐾 _____

🐾 _____

Tonight as I drift off to sleep I will send happiness & *pawsitive* thoughts to...

_____

The best vitamin to be a happy person is B1.

ANONYMOUS

Date _____

Pawsitive Power Word _____

am

This morning I woke up feeling _____ and I'd prefer to feel _____

I am grateful to my dog because _____

How can my BFF inspire me to have a more *pawsitive* day?

_____

_____

pm

3 *pawsitive* things that happened to me today were...

🐾 _____

🐾 _____

🐾 _____

Tonight as I drift off to sleep I will send happiness & *pawsitive* thoughts to...

_____

No matter how little money and how few possessions
you own, having a dog makes you rich.

LOUIS SABIN

Date _____

Pawsitive Power Word _____

am

This morning I woke up feeling _____ and I'd prefer to feel _____

I am grateful to my dog because _____

How can my BFF inspire me to have a more *pawsitive* day?

_____

_____

pm

3 *pawsitive* things that happened to me today were...

🐾 _____

🐾 _____

🐾 _____

Tonight as I drift off to sleep I will send happiness & *pawsitive* thoughts to...

_____

We can't direct the wind, but we can adjust the sails.

ANONYMOUS

Date _____

Pawsitive Power Word _____

am

This morning I woke up feeling _____ and I'd prefer to feel _____

I am grateful to my dog because _____

How can my BFF inspire me to have a more *pawsitive* day?

_____

_____

pm

3 *pawsitive* things that happened to me today were...

🐾 _____

🐾 _____

🐾 _____

Tonight as I drift off to sleep I will send happiness & *pawsitive* thoughts to...

_____

If I could be half the person my dog is, I'd be twice the human I am.

CHARLES YU

Date _____

Pawsitive Power Word _____

am

This morning I woke up feeling _____ and I'd prefer to feel _____

I am grateful to my dog because _____

How can my BFF inspire me to have a more *pawsitive* day?

_____

_____

pm

3 *pawsitive* things that happened to me today were...

🐾 _____

🐾 _____

🐾 _____

Tonight as I drift off to sleep I will send happiness & *pawsitive* thoughts to...

_____

Gather the crumbs of happiness and they will make you a loaf of contentment.
ANONYMOUS

The Seventh Day Challenge

How did you and your dog first meet?
What drew you to each other?

_____

_____

_____

_____

_____

_____

_____

_____

_____

_____

_____

_____

_____

_____

_____

Dogs are not our whole life, but they make our lives whole.

ROGER CARAS

Date _____

Pawsitive Power Word _____

am

This morning I woke up feeling _____ and I'd prefer to feel _____

I am grateful to my dog because _____

How can my BFF inspire me to have a more *pawsitive* day?

_____

_____

pm

3 *pawsitive* things that happened to me today were...

🐾 _____

🐾 _____

🐾 _____

Tonight as I drift off to sleep I will send happiness & *pawsitive* thoughts to...

_____

*True happiness comes not from a limited concern for one's
own well-being, or that of those one feels close to,
but from developing love and compassion for all sentient beings.*

HIS HOLINESS THE 14TH DALAI LAMA

Date _____

Pawsitive Power Word _____

am

This morning I woke up feeling _____ and I'd prefer to feel _____

I am grateful to my dog because _____

How can my BFF inspire me to have a more *pawsitive* day?

_____

_____

pm

3 *pawsitive* things that happened to me today were...

🐾 _____

🐾 _____

🐾 _____

Tonight as I drift off to sleep I will send happiness & *pawsitive* thoughts to...

_____

Those who teach the most about humanity, aren't always human.

DONALD L. HICKS

Date _____

Pawsitive Power Word _____

am

This morning I woke up feeling _____ and I'd prefer to feel _____

I am grateful to my dog because _____

How can my BFF inspire me to have a more *pawsitive* day?

_____

_____

pm

3 *pawsitive* things that happened to me today were...

🐾 _____

🐾 _____

🐾 _____

Tonight as I drift off to sleep I will send happiness & *pawsitive* thoughts to...

_____

Be a Fruit Loop in a world of Cheerios.

ANONYMOUS

Date _____

Pawsitive Power Word _____

am

This morning I woke up feeling _____ and I'd prefer to feel _____

I am grateful to my dog because _____

How can my BFF inspire me to have a more *pawsitive* day?

_____

_____

pm

3 *pawsitive* things that happened to me today were...

🐾 _____

🐾 _____

🐾 _____

Tonight as I drift off to sleep I will send happiness & *pawsitive* thoughts to...

_____

Until one has loved an animal, a part of one's soul remains unawakened.

ANATOLE FRANCE

Date _____

Pawsitive Power Word _____

am

This morning I woke up feeling _____ and I'd prefer to feel _____

I am grateful to my dog because _____

How can my BFF inspire me to have a more *pawsitive* day?

_____

_____

pm

3 *pawsitive* things that happened to me today were...

🐾 _____

🐾 _____

🐾 _____

Tonight as I drift off to sleep I will send happiness & *pawsitive* thoughts to...

_____

A heart full of joy is better than a hand full of coins.

MATSHONA DHLIWAYO

Date _____

Pawsitive Power Word _____

am

This morning I woke up feeling _____ and I'd prefer to feel _____

I am grateful to my dog because _____

How can my BFF inspire me to have a more *pawsitive* day?

_____

_____

pm

3 *pawsitive* things that happened to me today were...

🐾 _____

🐾 _____

🐾 _____

Tonight as I drift off to sleep I will send happiness & *pawsitive* thoughts to...

_____

There is no psychiatrist in the world like a puppy licking your face.

BERNARD WILLIAMS

The Seventh Day Challenge

If my dog could talk, what do I think she/he would want me to know?

So many of our dreams at first seem impossible,
then they seem improbable, and then, when we summon the will,
they soon become inevitable.

CHRISTOPHER REEVE

Date _____

Pawsitive Power Word _____

am

This morning I woke up feeling _____ and I'd prefer to feel _____

I am grateful to my dog because _____

How can my BFF inspire me to have a more *pawsitive* day?

_____

_____

pm

3 *pawsitive* things that happened to me today were...

🐾 _____

🐾 _____

🐾 _____

Tonight as I drift off to sleep I will send happiness & *pawsitive* thoughts to...

_____

I think dogs are the most amazing creatures; they give unconditional love.
For me they are the role model for being alive.

GILDA RADNER

Date _____

Pawsitive Power Word _____

am

This morning I woke up feeling _____ and I'd prefer to feel _____

I am grateful to my dog because _____

How can my BFF inspire me to have a more *pawsitive* day?

_____

_____

pm

3 *pawsitive* things that happened to me today were...

🐾 _____

🐾 _____

🐾 _____

Tonight as I drift off to sleep I will send happiness & *pawsitive* thoughts to...

_____

Don't cry because it's over, smile because it happened.

DR. SEUSS

Date _____

Pawsitive Power Word _____

am

This morning I woke up feeling _____ and I'd prefer to feel _____

I am grateful to my dog because _____

How can my BFF inspire me to have a more *pawsitive* day?

_____

_____

pm

3 *pawsitive* things that happened to me today were...

- _____
- _____
- _____

Tonight as I drift off to sleep I will send happiness & *pawsitive* thoughts to...

_____

All his life he tried to be a good person. Many times, however, he failed.
For after all, he was only human. He wasn't a dog.

CHARLES M. SCHULZ

Date _____

Pawsitive Power Word _____

am

This morning I woke up feeling _____ and I'd prefer to feel _____

I am grateful to my dog because _____

How can my BFF inspire me to have a more *pawsitive* day?

_____

_____

pm

3 *pawsitive* things that happened to me today were...

🐾 _____

🐾 _____

🐾 _____

Tonight as I drift off to sleep I will send happiness & *pawsitive* thoughts to...

_____

37

A laugh can be a very powerful thing.
Why, sometimes in life, it's the only weapon we have.

ROGER RABBIT

Date _____

Pawsitive Power Word _____

am

This morning I woke up feeling _____ and I'd prefer to feel _____

I am grateful to my dog because _____

How can my BFF inspire me to have a more *pawsitive* day?

_____

_____

pm

3 *pawsitive* things that happened to me today were...

🐾 _____

🐾 _____

🐾 _____

Tonight as I drift off to sleep I will send happiness & *pawsitive* thoughts to...

_____

The dog was created especially for children. He is the god of frolic.

HENRY WARD BEECHER

Date _____

Pawsitive Power Word _____

am

This morning I woke up feeling _____ and I'd prefer to feel _____

I am grateful to my dog because _____

How can my BFF inspire me to have a more *pawsitive* day?

_____

_____

pm

3 *pawsitive* things that happened to me today were...

🐾 _____

🐾 _____

🐾 _____

Tonight as I drift off to sleep I will send happiness & *pawsitive* thoughts to...

_____

In every day, there are 1,440 minutes. That means we have 1,440 daily opportunities to make a positive impact.

LES BROWN

The Seventh Day Challenge

List 5 *pawsitive* power words that best describe your dog.
List 5 *pawsitive* power words that best describe you.

1 _____   1 _____

2 _____   2 _____

3 _____   3 _____

4 _____   4 _____

5 _____   5 _____

Did you know...

Japanese researchers found that levels of oxytocin — a hormone that elicits feelings of happiness — increased after looking into our eyes?

Note: Not all of us dogs feel comfortable when you look into our eyes. Always take our cue. If we look away, that's ok, it's nothing personal. When we willingly allow your gaze, you have made a friend for life!

If having a soul means being able to feel love and loyalty and gratitude,
then animals are better off than a lot of humans.

JAMES HERRIOT

Date _____

Pawsitive Power Word _____

am

This morning I woke up feeling _____ and I'd prefer to feel _____

I am grateful to my dog because _____

How can my BFF inspire me to have a more *pawsitive* day?

_____

_____

pm

3 *pawsitive* things that happened to me today were...

🐾 _____

🐾 _____

🐾 _____

Tonight as I drift off to sleep I will send happiness & *pawsitive* thoughts to...

_____

You cannot prevent the birds of sadness from passing over your head,
but you can prevent their making a nest in your hair.

CHINESE PROVERB

Date _____

Pawsitive Power Word _____

am

This morning I woke up feeling _____ and I'd prefer to feel _____

I am grateful to my dog because _____

How can my BFF inspire me to have a more *pawsitive* day?

_____

_____

pm

3 *pawsitive* things that happened to me today were...

🐾 _____

🐾 _____

🐾 _____

Tonight as I drift off to sleep I will send happiness & *pawsitive* thoughts to...

_____

You think dogs will not be in heaven?
I tell you, they will be there long before any of us.

ROBERT LOUIS STEVENSON

Date _____

Pawsitive Power Word _____

am

This morning I woke up feeling _____ and I'd prefer to feel _____

I am grateful to my dog because _____

How can my BFF inspire me to have a more *pawsitive* day?

_____

_____

pm

3 *pawsitive* things that happened to me today were...

🐾 _____

🐾 _____

🐾 _____

Tonight as I drift off to sleep I will send happiness & *pawsitive* thoughts to...

_____

Happiness is the meaning and the purpose of life,
the whole aim and end of human existence.

ARISTOTLE

Date _____

Pawsitive Power Word _____

am

This morning I woke up feeling _____ and I'd prefer to feel _____

I am grateful to my dog because _____

How can my BFF inspire me to have a more *pawsitive* day?

_____

_____

pm

3 *pawsitive* things that happened to me today were...

🐾 _____

🐾 _____

🐾 _____

Tonight as I drift off to sleep I will send happiness & *pawsitive* thoughts to...

_____

Handle every stressful situation like a dog.
If you can't eat it or play with it, just pee on it and walk away.

ANONYMOUS

Date _____

Pawsitive Power Word _____

am

This morning I woke up feeling _____ and I'd prefer to feel _____

I am grateful to my dog because _____

How can my BFF inspire me to have a more *pawsitive* day?

_____

_____

pm

3 *pawsitive* things that happened to me today were...

🐾 _____

🐾 _____

🐾 _____

Tonight as I drift off to sleep I will send happiness & *pawsitive* thoughts to...

_____

Shine like the whole universe is yours.

RUMI

Date _____

Pawsitive Power Word _____

am

This morning I woke up feeling _____ and I'd prefer to feel _____

I am grateful to my dog because _____

How can my BFF inspire me to have a more *pawsitive* day?

_____

_____

pm

3 *pawsitive* things that happened to me today were...

🐾 _____

🐾 _____

🐾 _____

Tonight as I drift off to sleep I will send happiness & *pawsitive* thoughts to...

_____

The Pawsitive Monthly Milestone

Create a Memory!

Take a selfie of your BFF and you at your favorite spot.
Send it as a text to someone you appreciate. Or turn it into a fun card
and mail it to someone who can use a smile.

Place your selfie below

#PawsForTheGoodStuff 🐾 Spread the *Pawsitivity!*

Share your picture with your online community and use #PawsForTheGoodStuff.
Together we can change the world, one *pawsitive* moment at a time.

Dig Deeper!

Keep it Fresh!

You are in a groove, journaling every morning and evening and discovering new and exciting ways to feel grateful and happier. You are starting to embrace the power in the practice. But if you are also beginning to feel that things are getting a little repetitive then it's time to get specific.

LEARN MORE ON HOW TO KEEP IT FRESH AT

PawsForTheGoodStuff.com/DigDeeper

Watch my exclusive short video and discover how you can take your journaling experience to the next level.

What a wonderful life I've had! I only wish I'd realized it sooner.

COLETTE

Date _____

Pawsitive Power Word _____

am

This morning I woke up feeling _____ and I'd prefer to feel _____

I am grateful to my dog because _____

How can my BFF inspire me to have a more *pawsitive* day?

_____

_____

pm

3 *pawsitive* things that happened to me today were...

🐾 _____

🐾 _____

🐾 _____

Tonight as I drift off to sleep I will send happiness & *pawsitive* thoughts to...

_____

In order to really enjoy a dog, one doesn't merely try to train him to be semi-human.
The point of it is to open oneself to the possibility of becoming partly a dog.

EDWARD HOAGLAND

Date _____

Pawsitive Power Word _____

am

This morning I woke up feeling _____ and I'd prefer to feel _____

I am grateful to my dog because _____

How can my BFF inspire me to have a more *pawsitive* day?

_____

_____

pm

3 *pawsitive* things that happened to me today were...

🐾 _____

🐾 _____

🐾 _____

Tonight as I drift off to sleep I will send happiness & *pawsitive* thoughts to...

_____

*Perfect happiness is a beautiful sunset, the giggle of a grandchild,
the first snowfall. It's the little things that make happy
moments, not the grand events. Joy comes in sips, not gulps.*

SHARON DRAPER

Date _____

Pawsitive Power Word _____

am

This morning I woke up feeling _____ and I'd prefer to feel _____

I am grateful to my dog because _____

How can my BFF inspire me to have a more *pawsitive* day?

_____

_____

pm

3 *pawsitive* things that happened to me today were...

🐾 _____

🐾 _____

🐾 _____

Tonight as I drift off to sleep I will send happiness & *pawsitive* thoughts to...

_____

The reason a dog has so many friends
is that he wags his tail instead of his tongue.

ANONYMOUS

Date _____

Pawsitive Power Word _____

am

This morning I woke up feeling _____ and I'd prefer to feel _____

I am grateful to my dog because _____

How can my BFF inspire me to have a more *pawsitive* day?

_____

_____

pm

3 *pawsitive* things that happened to me today were...

🐾 _____

🐾 _____

🐾 _____

Tonight as I drift off to sleep I will send happiness & *pawsitive* thoughts to...

_____

If you want to be happy, be.

LEO TOLSTOY

Date _____

Pawsitive Power Word _____

am

This morning I woke up feeling _____ and I'd prefer to feel _____

I am grateful to my dog because _____

How can my BFF inspire me to have a more *pawsitive* day?

_____

_____

pm

3 *pawsitive* things that happened to me today were...

🐾 _____

🐾 _____

🐾 _____

Tonight as I drift off to sleep I will send happiness & *pawsitive* thoughts to...

_____

Animals bring love to our hearts, and warmth to our souls.

COLLEEN KLAUM

Date _____

Pawsitive Power Word _____

am

This morning I woke up feeling _____ and I'd prefer to feel _____

I am grateful to my dog because _____

How can my BFF inspire me to have a more *pawsitive* day?

_____

_____

pm

3 *pawsitive* things that happened to me today were...

🐾 _____

🐾 _____

🐾 _____

Tonight as I drift off to sleep I will send happiness & *pawsitive* thoughts to...

_____

Cheerfulness is what greases the axles of the world.
Don't go through life creaking.

H.W. BYLES

The Seventh Day Challenge

My dog does so much to make me happy.
How can I bring more happiness to my BFF today?

The most powerful antidepressant has four paws, fur, and a wagging tail.

ANONYMOUS

Date _____

Pawsitive Power Word _____

am

This morning I woke up feeling _____ and I'd prefer to feel _____

I am grateful to my dog because _____

How can my BFF inspire me to have a more *pawsitive* day?

_____

_____

pm

3 *pawsitive* things that happened to me today were...

🐾 _____

🐾 _____

🐾 _____

Tonight as I drift off to sleep I will send happiness & *pawsitive* thoughts to...

_____

The positive thinker sees the invisible,
feels the intangible, and achieves the impossible.

WINSTON S. CHURCHILL

Date _____

Pawsitive Power Word _____

am

This morning I woke up feeling _____ and I'd prefer to feel _____

I am grateful to my dog because _____

How can my BFF inspire me to have a more *pawsitive* day?

_____

_____

pm

3 *pawsitive* things that happened to me today were...

🐾 _____

🐾 _____

🐾 _____

Tonight as I drift off to sleep I will send happiness & *pawsitive* thoughts to...

_____

To err is human, to forgive, canine.
ANONYMOUS

Date _____

Pawsitive Power Word _____

am

This morning I woke up feeling _____ and I'd prefer to feel _____

I am grateful to my dog because _____

How can my BFF inspire me to have a more *pawsitive* day?

_____

_____

pm

3 *pawsitive* things that happened to me today were...

🐾 _____

🐾 _____

🐾 _____

Tonight as I drift off to sleep I will send happiness & *pawsitive* thoughts to...

_____

Every survival kit should include a sense of humor.
ANONYMOUS

Date _____

Pawsitive Power Word _____

am

This morning I woke up feeling _____ and I'd prefer to feel _____

I am grateful to my dog because _____

How can my BFF inspire me to have a more *pawsitive* day?

_____

_____

pm

3 *pawsitive* things that happened to me today were...

🐾 _____

🐾 _____

🐾 _____

Tonight as I drift off to sleep I will send happiness & *pawsitive* thoughts to...

_____

He is your friend, your partner, your defender, your dog. You are his life,
his love, his leader. He will be yours, faithful and true, to the last beat of his heart.
You owe it to him to be worthy of such devotion.

ANONYMOUS

Date _____

Pawsitive Power Word _____

am

This morning I woke up feeling _____ and I'd prefer to feel _____

I am grateful to my dog because _____

How can my BFF inspire me to have a more *pawsitive* day?

_____

_____

pm

3 *pawsitive* things that happened to me today were...

🐾 _____

🐾 _____

🐾 _____

Tonight as I drift off to sleep I will send happiness & *pawsitive* thoughts to...

_____

Happiness cannot be traveled to, owned, earned,
worn or consumed. Happiness is the spiritual experience of living
every minute with love, grace, and gratitude.

DENIS WAITLEY

Date _____

Pawsitive Power Word _____

am

This morning I woke up feeling _____ and I'd prefer to feel _____

I am grateful to my dog because _____

How can my BFF inspire me to have a more *pawsitive* day?

_____

_____

pm

3 *pawsitive* things that happened to me today were...

🐾 _____

🐾 _____

🐾 _____

Tonight as I drift off to sleep I will send happiness & *pawsitive* thoughts to...

_____

Animals are such agreeable friends —
they ask no questions, they pass no criticisms.

GEORGE ELIOT

The Seventh Day Challenge

List 7 ways your dog made you happy this week.

1 _____

2 _____

3 _____

4 _____

5 _____

6 _____

7 _____

A dog's nose, knows.
CARLYN MONTES DE OCA

Did you know...

Our amazing noses are like your fingerprints; both have unique patterns of ridges and creases. Just as no human fingerprint is the same, no two dogs have the same nose print.

Oh and by the way — our sense of smell is 10 – 100,000 stronger than yours.

There is no cosmetic for beauty like happiness.

LADY BLESSINGTON

Date _____

Pawsitive Power Word _____

am

This morning I woke up feeling _____ and I'd prefer to feel _____

I am grateful to my dog because _____

How can my BFF inspire me to have a more *pawsitive* day?

_____

_____

pm

3 *pawsitive* things that happened to me today were...

🐾 _____

🐾 _____

🐾 _____

Tonight as I drift off to sleep I will send happiness & *pawsitive* thoughts to...

_____

He could tell by the way animals walked that they were keeping time to some kind of music. Maybe it was the song in their own hearts that they walked to.

LAURA ADAMS ARMER

Date _____

Pawsitive Power Word _____

am

This morning I woke up feeling _____ and I'd prefer to feel _____

I am grateful to my dog because _____

How can my BFF inspire me to have a more *pawsitive* day?

_____

_____

pm

3 *pawsitive* things that happened to me today were...

🐾 _____

🐾 _____

🐾 _____

Tonight as I drift off to sleep I will send happiness & *pawsitive* thoughts to...

_____

66

A happy person is not a person in a certain set of circumstances,
but rather a person with a certain set of attitudes.

HUGH DOWNS

Date _____

Pawsitive Power Word _____

am

This morning I woke up feeling _____ and I'd prefer to feel _____

I am grateful to my dog because _____

How can my BFF inspire me to have a more *pawsitive* day?

_____

_____

pm

3 *pawsitive* things that happened to me today were...

🐾 _____

🐾 _____

🐾 _____

Tonight as I drift off to sleep I will send happiness & *pawsitive* thoughts to...

_____

Animals are the bridge between us and the beauty of all that is natural. They show us what's missing in our lives, and how to love ourselves more completely and unconditionally. They connect us back to who we are, and to the purpose of why we're here.

TRISHA McCAGH

Date _____

Pawsitive Power Word _____

am

This morning I woke up feeling _____ and I'd prefer to feel _____

I am grateful to my dog because _____

How can my BFF inspire me to have a more *pawsitive* day?

_____

_____

pm

3 *pawsitive* things that happened to me today were...

🐾 _____

🐾 _____

🐾 _____

Tonight as I drift off to sleep I will send happiness & *pawsitive* thoughts to...

_____

You live longer once you realize that any time spent being unhappy is wasted.

RUTH E. RENKL

Date _____

Pawsitive Power Word _____

am

This morning I woke up feeling _____ and I'd prefer to feel _____

I am grateful to my dog because _____

How can my BFF inspire me to have a more *pawsitive* day?

_____

_____

pm

3 *pawsitive* things that happened to me today were...

🐾 _____

🐾 _____

🐾 _____

Tonight as I drift off to sleep I will send happiness & *pawsitive* thoughts to...

_____

Happiness is a warm puppy.

CHARLES M. SCHULZ

Date _____

Pawsitive Power Word _____

am

This morning I woke up feeling _____ and I'd prefer to feel _____

I am grateful to my dog because _____

How can my BFF inspire me to have a more *pawsitive* day?

_____

_____

pm

3 *pawsitive* things that happened to me today were...

🐾 _____

🐾 _____

🐾 _____

Tonight as I drift off to sleep I will send happiness & *pawsitive* thoughts to...

_____

Joy has no cost.

MARIANNE WILLIAMSON

The Seventh Day Challenge

Have you ever noticed your BFF doesn't judge? What would
you do differently if you knew no one would ever judge you?

When I look into the eyes of an animal I do not see an animal.
I see a living being. I see a friend. I feel a soul.

A.D. WILLIAMS

Date _____

Pawsitive Power Word _____

am

This morning I woke up feeling _____ and I'd prefer to feel _____

I am grateful to my dog because _____

How can my BFF inspire me to have a more *pawsitive* day?

_____

_____

pm

3 *pawsitive* things that happened to me today were...

🐾 _____

🐾 _____

🐾 _____

Tonight as I drift off to sleep I will send happiness & *pawsitive* thoughts to...

_____

*Once you replace negative thoughts with positive ones,
you'll start having positive results.*

WILLIE NELSON

Date _____

Pawsitive Power Word _____

am

This morning I woke up feeling _____ and I'd prefer to feel _____

I am grateful to my dog because _____

How can my BFF inspire me to have a more *pawsitive* day?

_____

_____

pm

3 *pawsitive* things that happened to me today were...

🐾 _____

🐾 _____

🐾 _____

Tonight as I drift off to sleep I will send happiness & *pawsitive* thoughts to...

_____

If you think dogs can't count, try putting three dog biscuits
in your pocket and then give him only two of them.

PHIL PASTORET

Date _____

Pawsitive Power Word _____

am

This morning I woke up feeling _____ and I'd prefer to feel _____

I am grateful to my dog because _____

How can my BFF inspire me to have a more *pawsitive* day?

_____

_____

pm

3 *pawsitive* things that happened to me today were...

🐾 _____

🐾 _____

🐾 _____

Tonight as I drift off to sleep I will send happiness & *pawsitive* thoughts to...

_____

Nothing is impossible, the word itself says 'I'm possible!'
AUDREY HEPBURN

Date _____

Pawsitive Power Word _____

am

This morning I woke up feeling _____ and I'd prefer to feel _____

I am grateful to my dog because _____

How can my BFF inspire me to have a more *pawsitive* day?

_____

_____

pm

3 *pawsitive* things that happened to me today were...

🐾 _____

🐾 _____

🐾 _____

Tonight as I drift off to sleep I will send happiness & *pawsitive* thoughts to...

_____

Surround your children with animals, for they are the teachers with purity of heart.
ANONYMOUS

Date _____

Pawsitive Power Word _____

am

This morning I woke up feeling _____ and I'd prefer to feel _____

I am grateful to my dog because _____

How can my BFF inspire me to have a more *pawsitive* day?

_____

_____

pm

3 *pawsitive* things that happened to me today were...

🐾 _____

🐾 _____

🐾 _____

Tonight as I drift off to sleep I will send happiness & *pawsitive* thoughts to...

_____

Keep your face always toward the sunshine — and shadows will fall behind you.

WALT WHITMAN

Date _____

Pawsitive Power Word _____

am

This morning I woke up feeling _____ and I'd prefer to feel _____

I am grateful to my dog because _____

How can my BFF inspire me to have a more *pawsitive* day?

_____

_____

pm

3 *pawsitive* things that happened to me today were...

🐾 _____

🐾 _____

🐾 _____

Tonight as I drift off to sleep I will send happiness & *pawsitive* thoughts to...

_____

The Pawsitive Monthly Milestone

Enjoy an Adventure!

Take a walking tour of your town. Discover new places you and your dog can go that you may not have been aware of before. At lunchtime stop at a dog friendly café or have a picnic in the park. Relish your time together — and don't forget to take a selfie!

Place your selfie below

#PawsForTheGoodStuff 🐾 Spread the *Pawsitivity*!

Share your picture with your online community and use #PawsForTheGoodStuff.
Together we can change the world, one *pawsitive* moment at a time.

Dig Deeper!

Use Your Senses!

Last month you learned how to get more specific as you journal.
When we get specific, magic begins to happen in our daily life.
How about creating more magic? You can do this by waking up
to the world of your 5 senses.

LEARN MORE ON HOW TO USE YOUR SENSES AT

PawsForTheGoodStuff.com/DigDeeper

Watch my exclusive short video and discover how you
can take your journaling experience to the next level.

Happiness is not something you postpone for the future;
it is something you design for the present.

JIM ROHN

Date _____

Pawsitive Power Word _____

am

This morning I woke up feeling _____ and I'd prefer to feel _____

I am grateful to my dog because _____

How can my BFF inspire me to have a more *pawsitive* day?

_____

_____

pm

3 *pawsitive* things that happened to me today were...

🐾 _____

🐾 _____

🐾 _____

Tonight as I drift off to sleep I will send happiness & *pawsitive* thoughts to...

_____

All of the animals except for man know
that the principle business of life is to enjoy it.

SAMUEL BUTLER

Date _____

Pawsitive Power Word _____

am

This morning I woke up feeling _____ and I'd prefer to feel _____

I am grateful to my dog because _____

How can my BFF inspire me to have a more *pawsitive* day?

_____

_____

pm

3 *pawsitive* things that happened to me today were...

🐾 _____

🐾 _____

🐾 _____

Tonight as I drift off to sleep I will send happiness & *pawsitive* thoughts to...

_____

For every minute you are angry you lose sixty seconds of happiness.

RALPH WALDO EMERSON

Date _____

Pawsitive Power Word _____

am

This morning I woke up feeling _____ and I'd prefer to feel _____

I am grateful to my dog because _____

How can my BFF inspire me to have a more *pawsitive* day?

_____

_____

pm

3 *pawsitive* things that happened to me today were...

🐾 _____

🐾 _____

🐾 _____

Tonight as I drift off to sleep I will send happiness & *pawsitive* thoughts to...

_____

The best doctor in the world is a wet nose and a wagging tail.

JILL ROBINSON

Date _____

Pawsitive Power Word _____

am

This morning I woke up feeling _____ and I'd prefer to feel _____

I am grateful to my dog because _____

How can my BFF inspire me to have a more *pawsitive* day?

_____

_____

pm

3 *pawsitive* things that happened to me today were...

🐾 _____

🐾 _____

🐾 _____

Tonight as I drift off to sleep I will send happiness & *pawsitive* thoughts to...

_____

Count your age by friends, not years. Count your life by smiles, not tears.

JOHN LENNON

Date _____

Pawsitive Power Word _____

am

This morning I woke up feeling _____ and I'd prefer to feel _____

I am grateful to my dog because _____

How can my BFF inspire me to have a more *pawsitive* day?

_____

_____

pm

3 *pawsitive* things that happened to me today were...

🐾 _____

🐾 _____

🐾 _____

Tonight as I drift off to sleep I will send happiness & *pawsitive* thoughts to...

_____

Once you have had a wonderful dog, a life without one is a life diminished.

DEAN KOONTZ

Date _____

Pawsitive Power Word _____

am

This morning I woke up feeling _____ and I'd prefer to feel _____

I am grateful to my dog because _____

How can my BFF inspire me to have a more *pawsitive* day?

_____

_____

pm

3 *pawsitive* things that happened to me today were...

🐾 _____

🐾 _____

🐾 _____

Tonight as I drift off to sleep I will send happiness & *pawsitive* thoughts to...

_____

Love is the most powerful thing in the world,
and you know, what love brings is joy.

DJ KHALED

The Seventh Day Challenge

Jot down a *Pawsitive* Power word and create an affirmation from it.
An affirmation is a powerful and *pawsitive* statement that you repeat
such as, "I am healthy, happy, and extraordinary!" Use your affirmation
regularly, whole-heartedly, and get ready to feel even more *pawsitive!*

Pawsitive Power Word

Affirmation

A dog doesn't care if you're rich or poor, smart or dumb.
Give him your heart... and he'll give you his.

MILO GATHEMA

Date _____

Pawsitive Power Word _____

am

This morning I woke up feeling _____ and I'd prefer to feel _____

I am grateful to my dog because _____

How can my BFF inspire me to have a more *pawsitive* day?

_____

_____

pm

3 *pawsitive* things that happened to me today were...

🐾 _____

🐾 _____

🐾 _____

Tonight as I drift off to sleep I will send happiness & *pawsitive* thoughts to...

_____

The foolish man seeks happiness in the distance,
the wise grows it under his feet.

JAMES OPPENHEIM

Date _____

Pawsitive Power Word _____

am

This morning I woke up feeling _____ and I'd prefer to feel _____

I am grateful to my dog because _____

How can my BFF inspire me to have a more *pawsitive* day?

_____

_____

pm

3 *pawsitive* things that happened to me today were...

🐾 _____

🐾 _____

🐾 _____

Tonight as I drift off to sleep I will send happiness & *pawsitive* thoughts to...

_____

I'm convinced that petting a puppy is good luck.

MEG DONOHUE

Date _____

Pawsitive Power Word _____

am

This morning I woke up feeling _____ and I'd prefer to feel _____

I am grateful to my dog because _____

How can my BFF inspire me to have a more *pawsitive* day?

_____

_____

pm

3 *pawsitive* things that happened to me today were...

🐾 _____

🐾 _____

🐾 _____

Tonight as I drift off to sleep I will send happiness & *pawsitive* thoughts to...

_____

Try to be a rainbow in someone's cloud.

MAYA ANGELOU

Date _____

Pawsitive Power Word _____

am

This morning I woke up feeling _____ and I'd prefer to feel _____

I am grateful to my dog because _____

How can my BFF inspire me to have a more *pawsitive* day?

_____

_____

pm

3 *pawsitive* things that happened to me today were...

🐾 _____

🐾 _____

🐾 _____

Tonight as I drift off to sleep I will send happiness & *pawsitive* thoughts to...

_____

We may have pets, but when it comes
to unconditional love, they are the masters.

DONALD L. HICKS

Date _____

Pawsitive Power Word _____

am

This morning I woke up feeling _____ and I'd prefer to feel _____

I am grateful to my dog because _____

How can my BFF inspire me to have a more *pawsitive* day?

_____

_____

pm

3 *pawsitive* things that happened to me today were...

🐾 _____

🐾 _____

🐾 _____

Tonight as I drift off to sleep I will send happiness & *pawsitive* thoughts to...

_____

If you carry joy in your heart, you can heal any moment.

CARLOS SANTANA

Date _____

Pawsitive Power Word _____

am

This morning I woke up feeling _____ and I'd prefer to feel _____

I am grateful to my dog because _____

How can my BFF inspire me to have a more *pawsitive* day?

_____

_____

pm

3 *pawsitive* things that happened to me today were...

🐾 _____

🐾 _____

🐾 _____

Tonight as I drift off to sleep I will send happiness & *pawsitive* thoughts to...

_____

If there are no dogs in heaven, then when I die I want to go where they went.

WILL ROGERS

The Seventh Day Challenge

How does your dog inspire you to live your best life?

Did you know...

According to the American Heart Association, living with one of us can lower your risk of cardiovascular disease and increase your chances of surviving a heart attack. And when it comes to unconditional love is there anything better for healing your heart than our wagging tails, wet noses, and snuggles?

There is no such thing as the pursuit of happiness,
but there is the discovery of joy.

JOYCE GRENFELL

Date _____

Pawsitive Power Word _____

am

This morning I woke up feeling _____ and I'd prefer to feel _____

I am grateful to my dog because _____

How can my BFF inspire me to have a more *pawsitive* day?

_____

_____

pm

3 *pawsitive* things that happened to me today were...

🐾 _____

🐾 _____

🐾 _____

Tonight as I drift off to sleep I will send happiness & *pawsitive* thoughts to...

_____

All beings are much more similar than they are different.
We should be looking for the connection between ourselves, and our animal friends,
instead of what sets us apart. This is how we come to discover our humanity.

JANE GOODALL

Date _____

Pawsitive Power Word _____

am

This morning I woke up feeling _____ and I'd prefer to feel _____

I am grateful to my dog because _____

How can my BFF inspire me to have a more *pawsitive* day?

_____

_____

pm

3 *pawsitive* things that happened to me today were...

🐾 _____

🐾 _____

🐾 _____

Tonight as I drift off to sleep I will send happiness & *pawsitive* thoughts to...

_____

*Joy is what happens to us when we allow ourselves
to recognize how good things really are.*

MARIANNE WILLIAMSON

Date _____

Pawsitive Power Word _____

am

This morning I woke up feeling _____ and I'd prefer to feel _____

I am grateful to my dog because _____

How can my BFF inspire me to have a more *pawsitive* day?

_____

_____

pm

3 *pawsitive* things that happened to me today were...

🐾 _____

🐾 _____

🐾 _____

Tonight as I drift off to sleep I will send happiness & *pawsitive* thoughts to...

_____

Outside of a dog, a book is man's best friend.
Inside of a dog it's too dark to read.

GROUCHO MARX

Date _____

Pawsitive Power Word _____

am

This morning I woke up feeling _____ and I'd prefer to feel _____

I am grateful to my dog because _____

How can my BFF inspire me to have a more *pawsitive* day?

_____

_____

pm

3 *pawsitive* things that happened to me today were...

🐾 _____

🐾 _____

🐾 _____

Tonight as I drift off to sleep I will send happiness & *pawsitive* thoughts to...

_____

Positive anything is better than negative nothing.

Date _____

Pawsitive Power Word _____

am

This morning I woke up feeling _____ and I'd prefer to feel _____

I am grateful to my dog because _____

How can my BFF inspire me to have a more *pawsitive* day?

_____

_____

pm

3 *pawsitive* things that happened to me today were...

🐾 _____

🐾 _____

🐾 _____

Tonight as I drift off to sleep I will send happiness & *pawsitive* thoughts to...

_____

Such short little lives our pets have to spend with us,
and they spend most of it waiting for us to come home each day.

JOHN GROGAN

Date _____

Pawsitive Power Word _____

am

This morning I woke up feeling _____ and I'd prefer to feel _____

I am grateful to my dog because _____

How can my BFF inspire me to have a more *pawsitive* day?

_____

_____

pm

3 *pawsitive* things that happened to me today were...

🐾 _____

🐾 _____

🐾 _____

Tonight as I drift off to sleep I will send happiness & *pawsitive* thoughts to...

_____

When one door of happiness closes, another opens, but often we look so long at the closed door that we do not see the one that has been opened for us.

HELEN KELLER

The Seventh Day Challenge

What do you think your dog is feeling right now?
What are you feeling at this very moment?

Petting, scratching, and cuddling a dog could be as soothing to the mind and heart as deep meditation and almost as good for the soul as prayer.

DEAN KOONTZ

Date _____

Pawsitive Power Word _____

am

This morning I woke up feeling _____ and I'd prefer to feel _____

I am grateful to my dog because _____

How can my BFF inspire me to have a more *pawsitive* day?

_____

_____

pm

3 *pawsitive* things that happened to me today were...

🐾 _____

🐾 _____

🐾 _____

Tonight as I drift off to sleep I will send happiness & *pawsitive* thoughts to...

_____

Attitude is a little thing that makes a big difference.

WINSTON CHURCHILL

Date _____

Pawsitive Power Word _____

am

This morning I woke up feeling _____ and I'd prefer to feel _____

I am grateful to my dog because _____

How can my BFF inspire me to have a more *pawsitive* day?

_____

_____

pm

3 *pawsitive* things that happened to me today were...

🐾 _____

🐾 _____

🐾 _____

Tonight as I drift off to sleep I will send happiness & *pawsitive* thoughts to...

_____

An animal's eyes have the power to speak a great language.

MARTIN BUBER

Date _____

Pawsitive Power Word _____

am

This morning I woke up feeling _____ and I'd prefer to feel _____

I am grateful to my dog because _____

How can my BFF inspire me to have a more *pawsitive* day?

_____

_____

pm

3 *pawsitive* things that happened to me today were...

🐾 _____

🐾 _____

🐾 _____

Tonight as I drift off to sleep I will send happiness & *pawsitive* thoughts to...

_____

Sometimes your joy is the source of your smile,
but sometimes your smile can be the source of your joy.

THICH NHAT HANH

Date _____

Pawsitive Power Word _____

am

This morning I woke up feeling _____ and I'd prefer to feel _____

I am grateful to my dog because _____

How can my BFF inspire me to have a more *pawsitive* day?

_____

_____

pm

3 *pawsitive* things that happened to me today were...

🐾 _____

🐾 _____

🐾 _____

Tonight as I drift off to sleep I will send happiness & *pawsitive* thoughts to...

_____

My goal in life is to become as wonderful as my dog thinks I am.

TOBY & EILEEN GREEN

Date _____

Pawsitive Power Word _____

am

This morning I woke up feeling _____ and I'd prefer to feel _____

I am grateful to my dog because _____

How can my BFF inspire me to have a more *pawsitive* day?

_____

_____

pm

3 *pawsitive* things that happened to me today were...

🐾 _____

🐾 _____

🐾 _____

Tonight as I drift off to sleep I will send happiness & *pawsitive* thoughts to...

_____

Life is ten percent what happens to you and ninety percent how you respond to it.

LOU HOLTZ

Date _____

Pawsitive Power Word _____

am

This morning I woke up feeling _____ and I'd prefer to feel _____

I am grateful to my dog because _____

How can my BFF inspire me to have a more *pawsitive* day?

_____

_____

pm

3 *pawsitive* things that happened to me today were...

🐾 _____

🐾 _____

🐾 _____

Tonight as I drift off to sleep I will send happiness & *pawsitive* thoughts to...

_____

The Pawsitive Monthly Milestone

Give Your Bestie a Gift!

Visit your favorite pet store and pick up something for your BFF.
Don't make it expensive, your friend is sure to enjoy even the smallest treasure.
If you don't feel like shopping get creative and make something instead.
Take a picture of your BFF's reaction. It should be priceless.

Place your picture below

#PawsForTheGoodStuff 🐾 Spread the *Pawsitivity*!

Share your picture with your online community and use #PawsForTheGoodStuff.
Together we can change the world, one *pawsitive* moment at a time.

Dig Deeper!

How Does it Feel?

Last month you added the elements of sight, sound, smell, touch, and taste to create a richer journaling experience. Shall we take it up another notch? You can do that by getting out of your head and into your heart.

LEARN MORE ON HOW IT FEELS AT

PawsForTheGoodStuff.com/DigDeeper

Watch my exclusive short video and discover how you can take your journaling experience to the next level.

*I slept and dreamt that life was joy. I awoke and saw
that life was service. I acted and behold, service was joy.*

RABINDRANATH TAGORE

Date _____

Pawsitive Power Word _____

am

This morning I woke up feeling _____ and I'd prefer to feel _____

I am grateful to my dog because _____

How can my BFF inspire me to have a more *pawsitive* day?

_____

_____

pm

3 *pawsitive* things that happened to me today were...

🐾 _____

🐾 _____

🐾 _____

Tonight as I drift off to sleep I will send happiness & *pawsitive* thoughts to...

_____

110

Some of my best leading men have been dogs and horses.

ELIZABETH TAYLOR

Date _____

Pawsitive Power Word _____

am

This morning I woke up feeling _____ and I'd prefer to feel _____

I am grateful to my dog because _____

How can my BFF inspire me to have a more *pawsitive* day?

_____

_____

pm

3 *pawsitive* things that happened to me today were...

🐾 _____

🐾 _____

🐾 _____

Tonight as I drift off to sleep I will send happiness & *pawsitive* thoughts to...

_____

If you aren't grateful for what you already have,
what makes you think you would be happy with more.

ROY T. BENNETT

Date _____

Pawsitive Power Word _____

am

This morning I woke up feeling _____ and I'd prefer to feel _____

I am grateful to my dog because _____

How can my BFF inspire me to have a more *pawsitive* day?

_____

_____

pm

3 *pawsitive* things that happened to me today were...

🐾 _____

🐾 _____

🐾 _____

Tonight as I drift off to sleep I will send happiness & *pawsitive* thoughts to...

_____

Scratch a dog and you'll find a permanent job.

FRANKLIN P. JONES

Date _____

Pawsitive Power Word _____

am

This morning I woke up feeling _____ and I'd prefer to feel _____

I am grateful to my dog because _____

How can my BFF inspire me to have a more *pawsitive* day?

_____

_____

pm

3 *pawsitive* things that happened to me today were...

🐾 _____

🐾 _____

🐾 _____

Tonight as I drift off to sleep I will send happiness & *pawsitive* thoughts to...

_____

Folks are usually about as happy as they make their minds up to be.

ABRAHAM LINCOLN

Date _____

Pawsitive Power Word _____

am

This morning I woke up feeling _____ and I'd prefer to feel _____

I am grateful to my dog because _____

How can my BFF inspire me to have a more *pawsitive* day?

_____

_____

pm

3 *pawsitive* things that happened to me today were...

🐾 _____

🐾 _____

🐾 _____

Tonight as I drift off to sleep I will send happiness & *pawsitive* thoughts to...

_____

There is no faith which has never yet been broken,
except that of a truly faithful dog.

KONRAD LORENZ

Date _____

Pawsitive Power Word _____

am

This morning I woke up feeling _____ and I'd prefer to feel _____

I am grateful to my dog because _____

How can my BFF inspire me to have a more *pawsitive* day?

_____

_____

pm

3 *pawsitive* things that happened to me today were...

🐾 _____

🐾 _____

🐾 _____

Tonight as I drift off to sleep I will send happiness & *pawsitive* thoughts to...

_____

115

It is not how much we have, but how much we enjoy, that makes happiness.
CHARLES SPURGEON

The Seventh Day Challenge

Describe your favorite memory with your BFF.

You can usually tell that a man is good if he has a dog who loves him.

W. BRUCE CAMERON

Date _____

Pawsitive Power Word _____

am

This morning I woke up feeling _____ and I'd prefer to feel _____

I am grateful to my dog because _____

How can my BFF inspire me to have a more *pawsitive* day?

_____

_____

pm

3 *pawsitive* things that happened to me today were...

🐾 _____

🐾 _____

🐾 _____

Tonight as I drift off to sleep I will send happiness & *pawsitive* thoughts to...

_____

Follow your bliss and the universe will open doors where there were only walls.

JOSEPH CAMPBELL

Date _____

Pawsitive Power Word _____

am

This morning I woke up feeling _____ and I'd prefer to feel _____

I am grateful to my dog because _____

How can my BFF inspire me to have a more *pawsitive* day?

_____

_____

pm

3 *pawsitive* things that happened to me today were...

🐾 _____

🐾 _____

🐾 _____

Tonight as I drift off to sleep I will send happiness & *pawsitive* thoughts to...

_____

118

Dogs are our link to paradise. They don't know evil or jealousy or discontent.
To sit with a dog on a hillside on a glorious afternoon is to be
back in Eden, where doing nothing was not boring — it was peace.

MILAN KUNDERA

Date _____

Pawsitive Power Word _____

am

This morning I woke up feeling _____ and I'd prefer to feel _____

I am grateful to my dog because _____

How can my BFF inspire me to have a more *pawsitive* day?

_____

_____

pm

3 *pawsitive* things that happened to me today were...

🐾 _____

🐾 _____

🐾 _____

Tonight as I drift off to sleep I will send happiness & *pawsitive* thoughts to...

_____

The only disability in life is a bad attitude.

SCOTT HAMILTON

Date _____

Pawsitive Power Word _____

am

This morning I woke up feeling _____ and I'd prefer to feel _____

I am grateful to my dog because _____

How can my BFF inspire me to have a more *pawsitive* day?

_____

_____

pm

3 *pawsitive* things that happened to me today were...

🐾 _____

🐾 _____

🐾 _____

Tonight as I drift off to sleep I will send happiness & *pawsitive* thoughts to...

_____

When an eighty-five pound mammal licks your tears away,
then tries to sit on your lap, it's hard to feel sad.

KRISTAN HIGGINS

Date _____

Pawsitive Power Word _____

am

This morning I woke up feeling _____ and I'd prefer to feel _____

I am grateful to my dog because _____

How can my BFF inspire me to have a more *pawsitive* day?

_____

_____

pm

3 *pawsitive* things that happened to me today were...

🐾 _____

🐾 _____

🐾 _____

Tonight as I drift off to sleep I will send happiness & *pawsitive* thoughts to...

_____

Love is the joy of the good, the wonder of the wise,
the amazement of the Gods.

PLATO

Date _____

Pawsitive Power Word _____

am

This morning I woke up feeling _____ and I'd prefer to feel _____

I am grateful to my dog because _____

How can my BFF inspire me to have a more *pawsitive* day?

_____

_____

pm

3 *pawsitive* things that happened to me today were...

🐾 _____

🐾 _____

🐾 _____

Tonight as I drift off to sleep I will send happiness & *pawsitive* thoughts to...

_____

I have found that when you are deeply troubled, there are things you get from the silent devoted companionship of a dog that you can get from no other source.

DORIS DAY

The Seventh Day Challenge

What one thing stands between you and your happiness?
How can your BFF help you move through it?

Did you know...

Dogs are masters of empathy. We know when you are anxious and stressed. And when you cry, we try to make things right by licking your tears away. We also know when you feel confident, excited, and happy. Studies show we know your mood by looking at your expressions. Take the time to get to know us, and you will get to know yourself better too.

When we seek to discover the best in others,
we somehow bring out the best in ourselves.

WILLIAM ARTHUR WARD

Date _____

Pawsitive Power Word _____

am

This morning I woke up feeling _____ and I'd prefer to feel _____

I am grateful to my dog because _____

How can my BFF inspire me to have a more *pawsitive* day?

_____

_____

pm

3 *pawsitive* things that happened to me today were...

🐾 _____

🐾 _____

🐾 _____

Tonight as I drift off to sleep I will send happiness & *pawsitive* thoughts to...

_____

A dog teaches a boy fidelity, perseverance,
and to turn around three times before lying down.

JOSH BILLINGS

Date _____

Pawsitive Power Word _____

am

This morning I woke up feeling _____ and I'd prefer to feel _____

I am grateful to my dog because _____

How can my BFF inspire me to have a more *pawsitive* day?

_____

_____

pm

3 *pawsitive* things that happened to me today were...

🐾 _____

🐾 _____

🐾 _____

Tonight as I drift off to sleep I will send happiness & *pawsitive* thoughts to...

_____

It is never too late to be what you might have been.

GEORGE ELIOT

Date _____

Pawsitive Power Word _____

am

This morning I woke up feeling _____ and I'd prefer to feel _____

I am grateful to my dog because _____

How can my BFF inspire me to have a more *pawsitive* day?

_____

_____

pm

3 *pawsitive* things that happened to me today were...

🐾 _____

🐾 _____

🐾 _____

Tonight as I drift off to sleep I will send happiness & *pawsitive* thoughts to...

_____

I sometimes look into the face of my dog Stan and see a wistful sadness and existential angst, when all he is actually doing is slowly scanning the ceiling for flies.

MERRILL MARKOE

Date _____

Pawsitive Power Word _____

am

This morning I woke up feeling _____ and I'd prefer to feel _____

I am grateful to my dog because _____

How can my BFF inspire me to have a more *pawsitive* day?

_____

_____

pm

3 *pawsitive* things that happened to me today were...

🐾 _____

🐾 _____

🐾 _____

Tonight as I drift off to sleep I will send happiness & *pawsitive* thoughts to...

_____

Whoever is happy will make others happy too.

ANNE FRANK

Date _____

Pawsitive Power Word _____

am

This morning I woke up feeling _____ and I'd prefer to feel _____

I am grateful to my dog because _____

How can my BFF inspire me to have a more *pawsitive* day?

_____

_____

pm

3 *pawsitive* things that happened to me today were...

🐾 _____

🐾 _____

🐾 _____

Tonight as I drift off to sleep I will send happiness & *pawsitive* thoughts to...

_____

Dogs' lives are too short. Their only fault, really.

AGNES SLIGH TURNBULL

Date _____

Pawsitive Power Word _____

am

This morning I woke up feeling _____ and I'd prefer to feel _____

I am grateful to my dog because _____

How can my BFF inspire me to have a more *pawsitive* day?

_____

_____

pm

3 *pawsitive* things that happened to me today were...

🐾 _____

🐾 _____

🐾 _____

Tonight as I drift off to sleep I will send happiness & *pawsitive* thoughts to...

_____

You cannot have a positive life and a negative mind.

JOYCE MEYER

The Seventh Day Challenge

List 10 things (besides your dog) that make you smile.
Remember to look at this "Happy List" anytime you are feeling blue.

Dogs don't rationalize. They don't hold anything against a person.
They don't see the outside of a human but the inside of a human.

CESAR MILLAN

Date _____

Pawsitive Power Word _____

am

This morning I woke up feeling _____ and I'd prefer to feel _____

I am grateful to my dog because _____

How can my BFF inspire me to have a more *pawsitive* day?

_____

_____

pm

3 *pawsitive* things that happened to me today were...

🐾 _____

🐾 _____

🐾 _____

Tonight as I drift off to sleep I will send happiness & *pawsitive* thoughts to...

_____

*The best and most beautiful things in the world cannot be seen
or even touched — they must be felt with the heart.*

HELEN KELLER

Date _____

Pawsitive Power Word _____

am

This morning I woke up feeling _____ and I'd prefer to feel _____

I am grateful to my dog because _____

How can my BFF inspire me to have a more *pawsitive* day?

_____

_____

pm

3 *pawsitive* things that happened to me today were...

🐾 _____

🐾 _____

🐾 _____

Tonight as I drift off to sleep I will send happiness & *pawsitive* thoughts to...

_____

It's just the most amazing thing to love a dog, isn't it?
It makes our relationships with people seem as boring as a bowl of oatmeal.

JOHN GROGAN

Date _____

Pawsitive Power Word _____

am

This morning I woke up feeling _____ and I'd prefer to feel _____

I am grateful to my dog because _____

How can my BFF inspire me to have a more *pawsitive* day?

_____

_____

pm

3 *pawsitive* things that happened to me today were...

🐾 _____

🐾 _____

🐾 _____

Tonight as I drift off to sleep I will send happiness & *pawsitive* thoughts to...

_____

Worry never robs tomorrow of its sorrow, it only saps today of its joy.

LEO BUSCAGLIA

Date _____

Pawsitive Power Word _____

am

This morning I woke up feeling _____ and I'd prefer to feel _____

I am grateful to my dog because _____

How can my BFF inspire me to have a more *pawsitive* day?

_____

_____

pm

3 *pawsitive* things that happened to me today were...

🐾 _____

🐾 _____

🐾 _____

Tonight as I drift off to sleep I will send happiness & *pawsitive* thoughts to...

_____

Dogs are minor angels, and I don't mean that facetiously.
They love unconditionally, forgive immediately, are the truest of friends,
willing to do anything that makes us happy...

JONATHAN CARROLL

Date _____

Pawsitive Power Word _____

am

This morning I woke up feeling _____ and I'd prefer to feel _____

I am grateful to my dog because _____

How can my BFF inspire me to have a more *pawsitive* day?

_____

_____

pm

3 *pawsitive* things that happened to me today were...

🐾 _____

🐾 _____

🐾 _____

Tonight as I drift off to sleep I will send happiness & *pawsitive* thoughts to...

_____

Let your joy be in your journey — not in some distant goal.

TIM COOK

Date _____

Pawsitive Power Word _____

am

This morning I woke up feeling _____ and I'd prefer to feel _____

I am grateful to my dog because _____

How can my BFF inspire me to have a more *pawsitive* day?

_____

_____

pm

3 *pawsitive* things that happened to me today were...

🐾 _____

🐾 _____

🐾 _____

Tonight as I drift off to sleep I will send happiness & *pawsitive* thoughts to...

_____

The Pawsitive Monthly Milestone

Expand Your Imagination!

Lie on the couch or curl up in bed and read your favorite dog book — to your dog. Some dogs find the human voice reading aloud very comforting (or at least that's what people who have read *Dog as My Doctor, Cat as My Nurse* have told me). Enjoy reading to your BFF and don't forget to take that selfie!

Place your selfie below

#PawsForTheGoodStuff Spread the *Pawsitivity*!

Share your picture with your online community and use #PawsForTheGoodStuff. Together we can change the world, one *pawsitive* moment at a time.

Dig Deeper!

Recognizing Resistance

Are you feeling happier, more cheerful, and generally more *pawsitive*?
But are you also feeling lazy, bored, or struggling with your journal?
If so then you may be experiencing *resistance*.

Resistance sneaks up in our relationships and careers, and side
tracks us from our deepest desires. Learn to recognize and conquer
your resistance.

LEARN MORE ON RECOGNIZING RESISTANCE AT
PawsForTheGoodStuff.com/DigDeeper

Watch my exclusive short video and discover how you
can take your journaling experience to the next level.

Laughter and joy are part of the beauty of life.

DIOGO MORGADO

Date _____

Pawsitive Power Word _____

am

This morning I woke up feeling _____ and I'd prefer to feel _____

I am grateful to my dog because _____

How can my BFF inspire me to have a more *pawsitive* day?

_____

_____

pm

3 *pawsitive* things that happened to me today were...

🐾 _____

🐾 _____

🐾 _____

Tonight as I drift off to sleep I will send happiness & *pawsitive* thoughts to...

_____

After years of having a dog, you know him. You know the meaning
of his snuffs and grunts and barks. Every twitch of the ears is a question
or statement, every wag of the tail is an exclamation.

ROBERT McCAMMON

Date _____

Pawsitive Power Word _____

am

This morning I woke up feeling _____ and I'd prefer to feel _____

I am grateful to my dog because _____

How can my BFF inspire me to have a more *pawsitive* day?

_____

_____

pm

3 *pawsitive* things that happened to me today were...

🐾 _____

🐾 _____

🐾 _____

Tonight as I drift off to sleep I will send happiness & *pawsitive* thoughts to...

_____

Be happy for this moment. This moment is your life.

OMAR KHAYYAM

Date _____

Pawsitive Power Word _____

am

This morning I woke up feeling _____ and I'd prefer to feel _____

I am grateful to my dog because _____

How can my BFF inspire me to have a more *pawsitive* day?

_____

_____

pm

3 *pawsitive* things that happened to me today were...

🐾 _____

🐾 _____

🐾 _____

Tonight as I drift off to sleep I will send happiness & *pawsitive* thoughts to...

_____

Date _____

Pawsitive Power Word _____

am

This morning I woke up feeling _____ and I'd prefer to feel _____

I am grateful to my dog because _____

How can my BFF inspire me to have a more *pawsitive* day?

_____

_____

pm

3 *pawsitive* things that happened to me today were...

🐾 _____

🐾 _____

🐾 _____

Tonight as I drift off to sleep I will send happiness & *pawsitive* thoughts to...

_____

In order to carry a positive action we must develop here a positive vision.

HIS HOLINESS THE 14TH DALAI LAMA

Date _____

Pawsitive Power Word _____

am

This morning I woke up feeling _____ and I'd prefer to feel _____

I am grateful to my dog because _____

How can my BFF inspire me to have a more *pawsitive* day?

_____

_____

pm

3 *pawsitive* things that happened to me today were...

🐾 _____

🐾 _____

🐾 _____

Tonight as I drift off to sleep I will send happiness & *pawsitive* thoughts to...

_____

*People leave imprints on our lives, shaping who we become in much
the same way that a symbol is pressed into the page of a book to tell you who
it comes from. Dogs, however, leave paw prints on our lives and our souls,
which are as unique as fingerprints in every way.*

ASHLY LORENZANA

Date _____

Pawsitive Power Word _____

am

This morning I woke up feeling _____ and I'd prefer to feel _____

I am grateful to my dog because _____

How can my BFF inspire me to have a more *pawsitive* day?

_____

_____

pm

3 *pawsitive* things that happened to me today were...

🐾 _____

🐾 _____

🐾 _____

Tonight as I drift off to sleep I will send happiness & *pawsitive* thoughts to...

_____

Gratitude can transform common days into thanksgivings,
turn routine jobs into joy, and change ordinary opportunities into blessings.

WILLIAM ARTHUR WARD

The Seventh Day Challenge

If your dog were your doctor, what advice would she/he give you?

A dog will teach you unconditional love.
If you can have that in your life, things won't be too bad.

ROBERT WAGNER

Date _____

Pawsitive Power Word _____

am

This morning I woke up feeling _____ and I'd prefer to feel _____

I am grateful to my dog because _____

How can my BFF inspire me to have a more *pawsitive* day?

_____

_____

pm

3 *pawsitive* things that happened to me today were...

🐾 _____

🐾 _____

🐾 _____

Tonight as I drift off to sleep I will send happiness & *pawsitive* thoughts to...

_____

Positive thinking will let you do everything better than negative thinking will.

ZIG ZIGLAR

Date _____

Pawsitive Power Word _____

am

This morning I woke up feeling _____ and I'd prefer to feel _____

I am grateful to my dog because _____

How can my BFF inspire me to have a more *pawsitive* day?

_____

_____

pm

3 *pawsitive* things that happened to me today were...

🐾 _____

🐾 _____

🐾 _____

Tonight as I drift off to sleep I will send happiness & *pawsitive* thoughts to...

_____

Dogs are the magicians of the universe.

CLARISSA PINKOLA ESTÉS

Date _____

Pawsitive Power Word _____

am

This morning I woke up feeling _____ and I'd prefer to feel _____

I am grateful to my dog because _____

How can my BFF inspire me to have a more *pawsitive* day?

_____

_____

pm

3 *pawsitive* things that happened to me today were...

🐾 _____

🐾 _____

🐾 _____

Tonight as I drift off to sleep I will send happiness & *pawsitive* thoughts to...

_____

149

The best way to cheer yourself up is to try to cheer somebody else up.

MARK TWAIN

Date _____

Pawsitive Power Word _____

am

This morning I woke up feeling _____ and I'd prefer to feel _____

I am grateful to my dog because _____

How can my BFF inspire me to have a more *pawsitive* day?

_____

_____

pm

3 *pawsitive* things that happened to me today were...

🐾 _____

🐾 _____

🐾 _____

Tonight as I drift off to sleep I will send happiness & *pawsitive* thoughts to...

_____

They had buried him under our elm tree, they said —
yet this was not totally true. For he really lay buried in my heart.

WILLIE MORRIS

Date _____

Pawsitive Power Word _____

am

This morning I woke up feeling _____ and I'd prefer to feel _____

I am grateful to my dog because _____

How can my BFF inspire me to have a more *pawsitive* day?

_____

_____

pm

3 *pawsitive* things that happened to me today were...

🐾 _____

🐾 _____

🐾 _____

Tonight as I drift off to sleep I will send happiness & *pawsitive* thoughts to...

_____

Happiness can be found even in the darkest of times.
If one only remembers to turn on the light.

ALBUS DUMBLEDORE

Date _____

Pawsitive Power Word _____

am

This morning I woke up feeling _____ and I'd prefer to feel _____

I am grateful to my dog because _____

How can my BFF inspire me to have a more *pawsitive* day?

_____

_____

pm

3 *pawsitive* things that happened to me today were...

🐾 _____

🐾 _____

🐾 _____

Tonight as I drift off to sleep I will send happiness & *pawsitive* thoughts to...

_____

Happiness is where my dog is.

CARLYN MONTES DE OCA

The Seventh Day Challenge

Draw anything you want on this page.
Use a pen, pencil, or try crayons — let your creativity soar!

You can always teach a dog a new trick — even when that dog is a human.
RUDY FISCHER

Did you know...

You are never too old to play?
Play fuels your imagination,
stimulates your mind and makes
you feel young. Just look at us!
At any time of the day we love to
catch a ball, frolic in the grass, or
enjoy a chew toy. Our advice? Play
often, love lots, and howl with joy!

The more you feed your mind with positive thoughts,
the more you can attract great things into your life.

ROY T. BENNETT

Date _____

Pawsitive Power Word _____

am

This morning I woke up feeling _____ and I'd prefer to feel _____

I am grateful to my dog because _____

How can my BFF inspire me to have a more *pawsitive* day?

_____

_____

pm

3 *pawsitive* things that happened to me today were...

🐾 _____

🐾 _____

🐾 _____

Tonight as I drift off to sleep I will send happiness & *pawsitive* thoughts to...

_____

We should have respect for animals because it makes better human beings of us all.

JANE GOODALL

Date _____

Pawsitive Power Word _____

am

This morning I woke up feeling _____ and I'd prefer to feel _____

I am grateful to my dog because _____

How can my BFF inspire me to have a more *pawsitive* day?

_____

_____

pm

3 *pawsitive* things that happened to me today were...

🐾 _____

🐾 _____

🐾 _____

Tonight as I drift off to sleep I will send happiness & *pawsitive* thoughts to...

_____

156

Things turn out best for the people who make the best of the way things turn out.

ART LINKLETTER

Date _____

Pawsitive Power Word _____

am

This morning I woke up feeling _____ and I'd prefer to feel _____

I am grateful to my dog because _____

How can my BFF inspire me to have a more *pawsitive* day?

_____

_____

pm

3 *pawsitive* things that happened to me today were...

🐾 _____

🐾 _____

🐾 _____

Tonight as I drift off to sleep I will send happiness & *pawsitive* thoughts to...

_____

Because dogs let go of all their anger daily, hourly, and never let it fester.
They absolve and forgive with each passing minute. Every turn
of a corner is the opportunity for a clean slate. Every bounce of a ball
brings joy and the promise of a fresh chase.

STEVEN ROWLEY

Date _____

Pawsitive Power Word _____

am

This morning I woke up feeling _____ and I'd prefer to feel _____

I am grateful to my dog because _____

How can my BFF inspire me to have a more *pawsitive* day?

_____

_____

pm

3 *pawsitive* things that happened to me today were...

🐾 _____

🐾 _____

🐾 _____

Tonight as I drift off to sleep I will send happiness & *pawsitive* thoughts to...

_____

158

Happiness is not a station you arrive at, but a manner of traveling.

MARGARET LEE RUNBECK

Date _____

Pawsitive Power Word _____

am

This morning I woke up feeling _____ and I'd prefer to feel _____

I am grateful to my dog because _____

How can my BFF inspire me to have a more *pawsitive* day?

_____

_____

pm

3 *pawsitive* things that happened to me today were...

🐾 _____

🐾 _____

🐾 _____

Tonight as I drift off to sleep I will send happiness & *pawsitive* thoughts to...

_____

Unlike man, a dog lives every moment and dies only once.

TAPAN GHOSH

Date _____

Pawsitive Power Word _____

am

This morning I woke up feeling _____ and I'd prefer to feel _____

I am grateful to my dog because _____

How can my BFF inspire me to have a more *pawsitive* day?

_____

_____

pm

3 *pawsitive* things that happened to me today were...

🐾 _____

🐾 _____

🐾 _____

Tonight as I drift off to sleep I will send happiness & *pawsitive* thoughts to...

_____

He who lives in harmony with himself lives in harmony with the universe.

MARCUS AURELIUS

The Seventh Day Challenge

We often teach our dogs tricks. But they can also teach us a lot in return.
What is one new trick your dog can teach you today?

*Dogs are like that, I guess — they know
how to fix you without ever saying a word.*

CAROLINE GEORGES

Date _____

Pawsitive Power Word _____

am

This morning I woke up feeling _____ and I'd prefer to feel _____

I am grateful to my dog because _____

How can my BFF inspire me to have a more *pawsitive* day?

_____

_____

pm

3 *pawsitive* things that happened to me today were...

🐾 _____

🐾 _____

🐾 _____

Tonight as I drift off to sleep I will send happiness & *pawsitive* thoughts to...

_____

Focus on the journey, not the destination.
Joy is found not in finishing an activity but in doing it.

GREG ANDERSON

Date _____

Pawsitive Power Word _____

am

This morning I woke up feeling _____ and I'd prefer to feel _____

I am grateful to my dog because _____

How can my BFF inspire me to have a more *pawsitive* day?

_____

_____

pm

3 *pawsitive* things that happened to me today were...

🐾 _____

🐾 _____

🐾 _____

Tonight as I drift off to sleep I will send happiness & *pawsitive* thoughts to...

_____

Thorns may hurt you, men desert you, sunlight turn to fog;
but you're never friendless ever, if you have a dog.

DOUGLAS MALLOCH

Date _____

Pawsitive Power Word _____

am

This morning I woke up feeling _____ and I'd prefer to feel _____

I am grateful to my dog because _____

How can my BFF inspire me to have a more *pawsitive* day?

_____

_____

pm

3 *pawsitive* things that happened to me today were...

🐾 _____

🐾 _____

🐾 _____

Tonight as I drift off to sleep I will send happiness & *pawsitive* thoughts to...

_____

There is no way to happiness — happiness is the way.

THICH NHAT HANH

Date _____

Pawsitive Power Word _____

am

This morning I woke up feeling _____ and I'd prefer to feel _____

I am grateful to my dog because _____

How can my BFF inspire me to have a more *pawsitive* day?

_____

_____

pm

3 *pawsitive* things that happened to me today were...

🐾 _____

🐾 _____

🐾 _____

Tonight as I drift off to sleep I will send happiness & *pawsitive* thoughts to...

_____

When I held my new puppy in my arms, I broke down in tears. Because I had fallen in love. Not somewhat in love. Not partly in love. Not in a limited amount. I fell fully in love with a creature I had known for all of nine hours.

STEVEN ROWLEY

Date _____

Pawsitive Power Word _____

am

This morning I woke up feeling _____ and I'd prefer to feel _____

I am grateful to my dog because _____

How can my BFF inspire me to have a more *pawsitive* day?

_____

_____

pm

3 *pawsitive* things that happened to me today were...

🐾 _____

🐾 _____

🐾 _____

Tonight as I drift off to sleep I will send happiness & *pawsitive* thoughts to...

_____

166

Laughter is an instant vacation.

MILTON BERLE

Date _____

Pawsitive Power Word _____

am

This morning I woke up feeling _____ and I'd prefer to feel _____

I am grateful to my dog because _____

How can my BFF inspire me to have a more *pawsitive* day?

_____

_____

pm

3 *pawsitive* things that happened to me today were...

🐾 _____

🐾 _____

🐾 _____

Tonight as I drift off to sleep I will send happiness & *pawsitive* thoughts to...

_____

The Pawsitive Monthly Milestone

Explore More!

If you are used to taking your BFF on a daily walk, consider going for a hike today.
Enjoy your natural surroundings as your dog explores new stimuli.
Be sure to bring water and treats for both of you and poop bags — for your dog.
If hiking seems like too much, explore a new street, path, or find a park
to stroll in. Take a selfie to remember this day!

Place your selfie below

#PawsForTheGoodStuff 🐾 Spread the *Pawsitivity*!

Share your picture with your online community and use #PawsForTheGoodStuff.
Together we can change the world, one *pawsitive* moment at a time.

Dig Deeper!

Dig Deeper & Wider

Besides your dog, is there another animal that you feel grateful for?
A bird who sings at your window; an elephant whose strength you
admire; a cow whose gentle gaze has touched your heart? There are
many reasons to be grateful to all of the animals we share our amazing
world with. This month, focus on giving gratitude to other animals in
addition to your own.

LEARN MORE GO TO

PawsForTheGoodStuff.com/DigDeeper

Watch my exclusive short video and discover how
to take your journaling experience to the next level.

There is nothing truer in this world than the love of a good dog.

MIRA GRANT

Date _____

Pawsitive Power Word _____

am

This morning I woke up feeling _____ and I'd prefer to feel _____

I am grateful to my dog because _____

How can my BFF inspire me to have a more *pawsitive* day?

_____

_____

pm

3 *pawsitive* things that happened to me today were...

🐾 _____

🐾 _____

🐾 _____

Tonight as I drift off to sleep I will send happiness & *pawsitive* thoughts to...

_____

The really happy person is the one who can enjoy the scenery,
even when they have to take a detour.

JAMES HOPWOOD JEANS

Date _____

Pawsitive Power Word _____

am

This morning I woke up feeling _____ and I'd prefer to feel _____

I am grateful to my dog because _____

How can my BFF inspire me to have a more *pawsitive* day?

_____

_____

pm

3 *pawsitive* things that happened to me today were...

🐾 _____

🐾 _____

🐾 _____

Tonight as I drift off to sleep I will send happiness & *pawsitive* thoughts to...

_____

*The world would be a nicer place if everyone had
the ability to love as unconditionally as a dog.*

M.K. CLINTON

Date _____

Pawsitive Power Word _____

am

This morning I woke up feeling _____ and I'd prefer to feel _____

I am grateful to my dog because _____

How can my BFF inspire me to have a more *pawsitive* day?

_____

_____

pm

3 *pawsitive* things that happened to me today were...

🐾 _____

🐾 _____

🐾 _____

Tonight as I drift off to sleep I will send happiness & *pawsitive* thoughts to...

_____

If you want others to be happy, practice compassion.
If you want to be happy, practice compassion.

HIS HOLINESS THE 14TH DALAI LAMA

Date _____

Pawsitive Power Word _____

am

This morning I woke up feeling _____ and I'd prefer to feel _____

I am grateful to my dog because _____

How can my BFF inspire me to have a more *pawsitive* day?

_____

_____

pm

3 *pawsitive* things that happened to me today were...

🐾 _____

🐾 _____

🐾 _____

Tonight as I drift off to sleep I will send happiness & *pawsitive* thoughts to...

_____

"I'm not alone," said the boy. "I've got a puppy."

JANE THAYER

Date _____

Pawsitive Power Word _____

am

This morning I woke up feeling _____ and I'd prefer to feel _____

I am grateful to my dog because _____

How can my BFF inspire me to have a more *pawsitive* day?

_____

_____

pm

3 *pawsitive* things that happened to me today were...

🐾 _____

🐾 _____

🐾 _____

Tonight as I drift off to sleep I will send happiness & *pawsitive* thoughts to...

_____

Find joy in everything you choose to do. Every job, relationship, home...
it's your responsibility to love it, or change it.

CHUCK PALAHNIUK

The Seventh Day Challenge

They say laughter is the best medicine.
What does your dog do to make you laugh?

When I let go of who I am, I become who I might be.

LAO TZU

Date _____

Pawsitive Power Word _____

am

This morning I woke up feeling _____ and I'd prefer to feel _____

I am grateful to my dog because _____

How can my BFF inspire me to have a more *pawsitive* day?

_____

_____

pm

3 *pawsitive* things that happened to me today were...

🐾 _____

🐾 _____

🐾 _____

Tonight as I drift off to sleep I will send happiness & *pawsitive* thoughts to...

_____

I love to think of nature as an unlimited broadcasting station,
through which God speaks to us every hour, if we will only tune in.

GEORGE WASHINGTON CARVER

Date _____

Pawsitive Power Word _____

am

This morning I woke up feeling _____ and I'd prefer to feel _____

I am grateful to my dog because _____

How can my BFF inspire me to have a more *pawsitive* day?

_____

_____

pm

3 *pawsitive* things that happened to me today were...

🐾 _____

🐾 _____

🐾 _____

Tonight as I drift off to sleep I will send happiness & *pawsitive* thoughts to...

_____

Did you know...

Rejection may not sting as much when you have a wagging tail by your side. A study found dog guardians not only have higher self-esteem but they bounce back from rejection better than non-dog guardians. No wonder we are man's best friend — and woman's too!

Some people talk to animals. Not many listen though. That's the problem.

A.A. MILNE

Date _____

Pawsitive Power Word _____

am

This morning I woke up feeling _____ and I'd prefer to feel _____

I am grateful to my dog because _____

How can my BFF inspire me to have a more *pawsitive* day?

_____

_____

pm

3 *pawsitive* things that happened to me today were...

🐾 _____

🐾 _____

🐾 _____

Tonight as I drift off to sleep I will send happiness & *pawsitive* thoughts to...

_____

Clouds come floating into my life, no longer to carry rain
or usher storm, but to add color to my sunset sky.

RABINDRANATH TAGORE

Date _____

Pawsitive Power Word _____

am

This morning I woke up feeling _____ and I'd prefer to feel _____

I am grateful to my dog because _____

How can my BFF inspire me to have a more *pawsitive* day?

_____

_____

pm

3 *pawsitive* things that happened to me today were...

🐾 _____

🐾 _____

🐾 _____

Tonight as I drift off to sleep I will send happiness & *pawsitive* thoughts to...

_____

Dogs, for a reason that can only be described as divine,
have the ability to forgive, let go of the past, and live each day joyously.
It's something the rest of us strive for.

JENNIFER SKIFF

Date _____

Pawsitive Power Word _____

am

This morning I woke up feeling _____ and I'd prefer to feel _____

I am grateful to my dog because _____

How can my BFF inspire me to have a more *pawsitive* day?

_____

_____

pm

3 *pawsitive* things that happened to me today were...

🐾 _____

🐾 _____

🐾 _____

Tonight as I drift off to sleep I will send happiness & *pawsitive* thoughts to...

_____

Yesterday I was clever, so I wanted to change the world.
Today I am wise, so I am changing myself.

RUMI

Date _____

Pawsitive Power Word _____

am

This morning I woke up feeling _____ and I'd prefer to feel _____

I am grateful to my dog because _____

How can my BFF inspire me to have a more *pawsitive* day?

_____

_____

pm

3 *pawsitive* things that happened to me today were...

🐾 _____

🐾 _____

🐾 _____

Tonight as I drift off to sleep I will send happiness & *pawsitive* thoughts to...

_____

*You know, a dog can snap you out of any kind of bad mood
that you're in faster than you can think of.*

JILL ABRAMSON

The Seventh Day Challenge

Dogs get excited over the simplest things.
What gets you excited about life?

We needed something to express our joy,
our beauty, our power. And the rainbow did that.

GILBERT BAKER

Date _____

Pawsitive Power Word _____

am

This morning I woke up feeling _____ and I'd prefer to feel _____

I am grateful to my dog because _____

How can my BFF inspire me to have a more *pawsitive* day?

_____

_____

pm

3 *pawsitive* things that happened to me today were...

🐾 _____

🐾 _____

🐾 _____

Tonight as I drift off to sleep I will send happiness & *pawsitive* thoughts to...

_____

184

For me a house or an apartment becomes a home when you add one set of four legs,
a happy tail, and that indescribable measure of love that we call a dog.

ROGER CARAS

Date _____

Pawsitive Power Word _____

am

This morning I woke up feeling _____ and I'd prefer to feel _____

I am grateful to my dog because _____

How can my BFF inspire me to have a more *pawsitive* day?

_____

_____

pm

3 *pawsitive* things that happened to me today were...

🐾 _____

🐾 _____

🐾 _____

Tonight as I drift off to sleep I will send happiness & *pawsitive* thoughts to...

_____

If you want to be happy, set a goal that commands your thoughts, liberates your energy, and inspires your hopes.

ANDREW CARNEGIE

Date _____

Pawsitive Power Word _____

am

This morning I woke up feeling _____ and I'd prefer to feel _____

I am grateful to my dog because _____

How can my BFF inspire me to have a more *pawsitive* day?

_____

_____

pm

3 *pawsitive* things that happened to me today were...

🐾 _____

🐾 _____

🐾 _____

Tonight as I drift off to sleep I will send happiness & *pawsitive* thoughts to...

_____

Dogs have a way of finding the people who need them,
and filling the emptiness we didn't ever know we had.

THOM JONES

Date _____

Pawsitive Power Word _____

am

This morning I woke up feeling _____ and I'd prefer to feel _____

I am grateful to my dog because _____

How can my BFF inspire me to have a more *pawsitive* day?

_____

_____

pm

3 *pawsitive* things that happened to me today were...

🐾 _____

🐾 _____

🐾 _____

Tonight as I drift off to sleep I will send happiness & *pawsitive* thoughts to...

_____

God, grant me the serenity to accept the things I cannot change,
the courage to change the things I can, and the wisdom to know the difference.

REINHOLD NIEBUHR

Date _____

Pawsitive Power Word _____

am

This morning I woke up feeling _____ and I'd prefer to feel _____

I am grateful to my dog because _____

How can my BFF inspire me to have a more *pawsitive* day?

_____

_____

pm

3 *pawsitive* things that happened to me today were...

🐾 _____

🐾 _____

🐾 _____

Tonight as I drift off to sleep I will send happiness & *pawsitive* thoughts to...

_____

Everyone thinks they have the best dog. And none of them are wrong.

W.R. PURCHE

Date _____

Pawsitive Power Word _____

am

This morning I woke up feeling _____ and I'd prefer to feel _____

I am grateful to my dog because _____

How can my BFF inspire me to have a more *pawsitive* day?

_____

_____

pm

3 *pawsitive* things that happened to me today were...

🐾 _____

🐾 _____

🐾 _____

Tonight as I drift off to sleep I will send happiness & *pawsitive* thoughts to...

_____

There is more to life than increasing its speed.
MAHATMA GANDHI

The Seventh Day Challenge

What is your dog great at? What are you great at?

Dogs never lie about love.

JEFFERY MASSON

Date _____

Pawsitive Power Word _____

am

This morning I woke up feeling _____ and I'd prefer to feel _____

I am grateful to my dog because _____

How can my BFF inspire me to have a more *pawsitive* day?

_____

_____

pm

3 *pawsitive* things that happened to me today were...

🐾 _____

🐾 _____

🐾 _____

Tonight as I drift off to sleep I will send happiness & *pawsitive* thoughts to...

_____

It is always the simple that produces the marvelous.

AMELIA BARR

Date _____

Pawsitive Power Word _____

am

This morning I woke up feeling _____ and I'd prefer to feel _____

I am grateful to my dog because _____

How can my BFF inspire me to have a more *pawsitive* day?

_____

_____

pm

3 *pawsitive* things that happened to me today were...

🐾 _____

🐾 _____

🐾 _____

Tonight as I drift off to sleep I will send happiness & *pawsitive* thoughts to...

_____

Everything I know I learned from dogs.

NORA ROBERTS

Date _____

Pawsitive Power Word _____

am

This morning I woke up feeling _____ and I'd prefer to feel _____

I am grateful to my dog because _____

How can my BFF inspire me to have a more *pawsitive* day?

_____

_____

pm

3 *pawsitive* things that happened to me today were...

🐾 _____

🐾 _____

🐾 _____

Tonight as I drift off to sleep I will send happiness & *pawsitive* thoughts to...

_____

Letting go means to come to the realization that some people
are a part of your history, but not a part of your destiny.

STEVE MARABOLI

Date _____

Pawsitive Power Word _____

am

This morning I woke up feeling _____ and I'd prefer to feel _____

I am grateful to my dog because _____

How can my BFF inspire me to have a more *pawsitive* day?

_____

_____

pm

3 *pawsitive* things that happened to me today were...

🐾 _____

🐾 _____

🐾 _____

Tonight as I drift off to sleep I will send happiness & *pawsitive* thoughts to...

_____

*Without my dog my wallet would be full my house
would be clean but my heart would be empty.*

ANONYMOUS

Date _____

Pawsitive Power Word _____

am

This morning I woke up feeling _____ and I'd prefer to feel _____

I am grateful to my dog because _____

How can my BFF inspire me to have a more *pawsitive* day?

_____

_____

pm

3 *pawsitive* things that happened to me today were...

🐾 _____

🐾 _____

🐾 _____

Tonight as I drift off to sleep I will send happiness & *pawsitive* thoughts to...

_____

In the end, only three things matter: how much you loved, how gently you lived, and how gracefully you let go of things not meant for you.

JACK KORNFIELD

Date _____

Pawsitive Power Word _____

am

This morning I woke up feeling _____ and I'd prefer to feel _____

I am grateful to my dog because _____

How can my BFF inspire me to have a more *pawsitive* day?

_____

_____

pm

3 *pawsitive* things that happened to me today were...

🐾 _____

🐾 _____

🐾 _____

Tonight as I drift off to sleep I will send happiness & *pawsitive* thoughts to...

_____

The Pawsitive Monthly Milestone

Make New Friends!

Friends are important for health, happiness, and longevity.
If you share your gratitude and *pawsitivity* with others, you and your dog
will be welcome members of many communities. Go to Meetup.com,
search for dog lovin' groups, and attend an event in your area. Take a selfie
of you, your new friends, and don't forget to include your BFF too!

Place your selfie below

#PawsForTheGoodStuff 🐾 Spread the *Pawsitivity*!

Share your picture with your online community and use #PawsForTheGoodStuff.
Together we can change the world, one *pawsitive* moment at a time.

"

We give dogs time we can spare,
space we can spare and love we can spare.
In return, dogs give us their all.
It's the best deal man has ever made.

MARGERY FACKLAM

Note to Self

Woohoo — I have two whole *bonus weeks* of journaling coming up!
Boohoo — I *only* have two weeks of journaling left!

It's time to order another copy of *Paws for the Good Stuff*
online or from my favorite bookstore!

A dog is the only thing that can mend a crack in your broken heart.

JUDY DESMOND

Date _____

Pawsitive Power Word _____

am

This morning I woke up feeling _____ and I'd prefer to feel _____

I am grateful to my dog because _____

How can my BFF inspire me to have a more *pawsitive* day?

_____

_____

pm

3 *pawsitive* things that happened to me today were...

🐾 _____

🐾 _____

🐾 _____

Tonight as I drift off to sleep I will send happiness & *pawsitive* thoughts to...

_____

If you know you are going to fail then fail gloriously!

CATE BLANCHETT

Date _____

Pawsitive Power Word _____

am

This morning I woke up feeling _____ and I'd prefer to feel _____

I am grateful to my dog because _____

How can my BFF inspire me to have a more *pawsitive* day?

_____

_____

pm

3 *pawsitive* things that happened to me today were...

🐾 _____

🐾 _____

🐾 _____

Tonight as I drift off to sleep I will send happiness & *pawsitive* thoughts to...

_____

I cannot imagine not going home to animals.
They are the closest thing to God; they don't harbor resentment.

ELLEN DEGENERES

Date _____

Pawsitive Power Word _____

am

This morning I woke up feeling _____ and I'd prefer to feel _____

I am grateful to my dog because _____

How can my BFF inspire me to have a more *pawsitive* day?

_____

_____

pm

3 *pawsitive* things that happened to me today were...

🐾 _____

🐾 _____

🐾 _____

Tonight as I drift off to sleep I will send happiness & *pawsitive* thoughts to...

_____

Shoot for the moon and if you miss you will still be among the stars.

LES BROWN

Date _____

Pawsitive Power Word _____

am

This morning I woke up feeling _____ and I'd prefer to feel _____

I am grateful to my dog because _____

How can my BFF inspire me to have a more *pawsitive* day?

_____

_____

pm

3 *pawsitive* things that happened to me today were...

🐾 _____

🐾 _____

🐾 _____

Tonight as I drift off to sleep I will send happiness & *pawsitive* thoughts to...

_____

My little dog — a heartbeat at my feet.

EDITH WHARTON

Date _____

Pawsitive Power Word _____

am

This morning I woke up feeling _____ and I'd prefer to feel _____

I am grateful to my dog because _____

How can my BFF inspire me to have a more *pawsitive* day?

_____

_____

pm

3 *pawsitive* things that happened to me today were...

🐾 _____

🐾 _____

🐾 _____

Tonight as I drift off to sleep I will send happiness & *pawsitive* thoughts to...

_____

In the end, it's not the years in your life that count. It's the life in your years.

ABRAHAM LINCOLN

Date _____

Pawsitive Power Word _____

am

This morning I woke up feeling _____ and I'd prefer to feel _____

I am grateful to my dog because _____

How can my BFF inspire me to have a more *pawsitive* day?

_____

_____

pm

3 *pawsitive* things that happened to me today were...

🐾 _____

🐾 _____

🐾 _____

Tonight as I drift off to sleep I will send happiness & *pawsitive* thoughts to...

_____

I have a very old and very faithful attachment for dogs.
I like them because they always forgive.

ALBERT CAMUS

The Seventh Day Challenge

Dogs give so much to those they love.
What is something you can do to brighten someone else's day?

i'm going to surprise my friend with dinner!

Your present circumstances don't determine where you can go;
they merely determine where you start.

NIDO QUBEIN

Date _____

Pawsitive Power Word _____

am

This morning I woke up feeling _____ and I'd prefer to feel _____

I am grateful to my dog because _____

How can my BFF inspire me to have a more *pawsitive* day?

_____

_____

pm

3 *pawsitive* things that happened to me today were...

🐾 _____

🐾 _____

🐾 _____

Tonight as I drift off to sleep I will send happiness & *pawsitive* thoughts to...

_____

Heaven is a place where all the dogs you've ever loved come to greet you.

OLIVER GASPIRTZ

Date _____

Pawsitive Power Word _____

am

This morning I woke up feeling _____ and I'd prefer to feel _____

I am grateful to my dog because _____

How can my BFF inspire me to have a more *pawsitive* day?

_____

_____

pm

3 *pawsitive* things that happened to me today were...

🐾 _____

🐾 _____

🐾 _____

Tonight as I drift off to sleep I will send happiness & *pawsitive* thoughts to...

_____

If you're feeling low, don't despair. The sun has a sinking spell
every night, but it comes back up every morning.

DOLLY PARTON

Date _____

Pawsitive Power Word _____

am

This morning I woke up feeling _____ and I'd prefer to feel _____

I am grateful to my dog because _____

How can my BFF inspire me to have a more *pawsitive* day?

_____

_____

pm

3 *pawsitive* things that happened to me today were...

🐾 _____

🐾 _____

🐾 _____

Tonight as I drift off to sleep I will send happiness & *pawsitive* thoughts to...

_____

I am the master of my fate: I am the captain of my soul.

WILLIAM ERNEST HENLEY

Date _____

Pawsitive Power Word _____

am

This morning I woke up feeling _____ and I'd prefer to feel _____

I am grateful to my dog because _____

How can my BFF inspire me to have a more *pawsitive* day?

_____

_____

pm

3 *pawsitive* things that happened to me today were...

🐾 _____

🐾 _____

🐾 _____

Tonight as I drift off to sleep I will send happiness & *pawsitive* thoughts to...

_____

Today I choose to feel life, not to deny my humanity but embrace it.
KEVYN AUCOIN

Date _____

Pawsitive Power Word _____

am

This morning I woke up feeling _____ and I'd prefer to feel _____

I am grateful to my dog because _____

How can my BFF inspire me to have a more *pawsitive* day?

_____

_____

pm

3 *pawsitive* things that happened to me today were...

🐾 _____

🐾 _____

🐾 _____

Tonight as I drift off to sleep I will send happiness & *pawsitive* thoughts to...

_____

Dogs die. But dogs live, too. Right up until they die, they live. They live brave, beautiful lives. They protect their families. And love us. And make our lives a little brighter. And they don't waste time being afraid of tomorrow.

DAN GEMEINHART

Date _____

Pawsitive Power Word _____

am

This morning I woke up feeling _____ and I'd prefer to feel _____

I am grateful to my dog because _____

How can my BFF inspire me to have a more *pawsitive* day?

_____

_____

pm

3 *pawsitive* things that happened to me today were...

🐾 _____

🐾 _____

🐾 _____

Tonight as I drift off to sleep I will send happiness & *pawsitive* thoughts to...

_____

True happiness comes from the joy of deeds well done, the zest of creating things new.

ANTOINE DE SAINT-EXUPERY

The Seventh Day Challenge

Dogs have a tremendous capacity to forgive.
Who do you need to forgive today?

The Pawsitive Monthly Milestone

Take a Pet Pawsitive Moment!

Take a few deep breaths to settle your mind. Then gently place your hand over your dog's paw. If your dog doesn't like his/her paw held, then just sit quietly beside your friend. Let your heart speak without saying a word and for the next two minutes send your dog all your love and gratitude.

Take a few moments to write about how your experience felt

My Pawsitive Notes

My Pawsitive Notes

My Pawsitive Notes

My Pawsitive Notes

My Pawsitive Notes

My Pawsitive Notes

My Pawsitive Notes

My Pawsitive Notes

My Pawsitive Notes

My Pawsitive Notes

Author Musings

I dearly hope *Paws for the Good Stuff* has enriched your life, shown you what is possible, and created a stronger bond between you and your dog.

My mission is to have the greatest *pawsitive* effect on the lives of animals and the humans who love them. Animals do so much for their human friends but it can't all be one sided; we need to help our animal friends too. And not just the ones in our home but chickens, cows, bears, gorillas and all sentient creatures we share our magnificent planet with. We are their voice, we are their hope, and together we can make a difference. So please...

🐾 Adopt don't shop   🐾 Be a guardian, not an owner   🐾 Go vegan

If you love animals as much as I do and want the best for them, then we are members of the same tribe. Let's connect!

Join me at ***PawsForTheGoodStuff.com*** to receive inspiring blog posts (I think you will really like them), helpful tips (who doesn't want to make their life better?) and be the first to find out about my new book releases (there's a lot more fun to come).

May your life's journey continue to be enhanced, empowered, and inspired by your fabulous relationships with your animal friends.

Stay *Pawsitive*,

EmDO

P.S. If you enjoyed *Paws for the Good Stuff*, please leave a review on Amazon.com or Goodreads.com so other dog lovers can enjoy it too!

About the Author

Carlyn Montes De Oca was born loving animals. And from her early days she realized they have a lot to teach humans about, well... being more human.

Besides being a best-selling award-winning author, Carlyn is also an acupuncturist, keynote speaker, wellness coach, plant-based nutritional consultant, movie buff, and animal advocate.

She holds a bachelor's degree from Loyola Marymount University in communication arts, a master's degree in Traditional Chinese Medicine from Emperor's College and is certified in plant-based nutrition from the T. Colin Campbell Center for Nutritional Studies at Cornell University.

Carlyn has been featured on television, radio, and dozens of media including ABC, CBS, Fox TV, AARP, and The San Francisco Chronicle.

Voted PETA's Sexiest Vegetarian Over 50 in 2011, Carlyn has been a spokesperson for the Guardian Campaign at In Defense of Animals.

Carlyn offers workshops, webinars, and private health and wellness coaching. As the founder of The Animal-Human Health Connection, she frequently speaks to community groups, animal shelters, non-profits, and corporations on the powerful ways we can improve health, happiness, and longevity through our connection to our animal companions.

Carlyn's mission is to have the greatest *pawsitive* effect on the lives of animals and the humans who love them. A California native, she now lives in Santa Fe, New Mexico with her husband Ken Fischer, an award-winning sound editor, and her beloved rescue animals.

Photo by Kevin Layton

Connect with Carlyn

Website AnimalHumanHealth.com
Email cmdo@AnimalHumanHealth.com
Facebook Carlyn Montes De Oca
Twitter CarlynMDO
Instagram CarlynMontesDeOca
Youtube Carlyn555

An excerpt from

Dog as My Doctor, Cat as My Nurse

Chapter 15

...With a house full of cats and dogs, I could not bring another animal into our home without upsetting the balance of the other two and four legged creatures in my life. But when I met Mack and saw his situation, I could not turn my back on him. As Mack braved going out of his own comfort zone, this unforgettable dog led me out of mine.

Mack & Carlyn

He reminded me of Cujo: the rabid dog in the horror movie by Stephen King. At the shelter where I volunteered, when the dogs saw a human, they would run up to the front of their cages, desperate for affection and hoping to be walked — but not Mack. He would slink to the back of his enclosure and his massive, eighty-five pound, black lab-pit bull body would disappear into the darkness. No one wanted to go near him.

Eventually, I'd had enough. I could no longer bear to see Mack in his cage, unwalked, unloved, and passed over for adoption week after week. My concern for him outweighed my fear of him, so I took a deep breath, opened his cage, and stepped inside.

I was nervous at first but decided it was a good day to 'fake it until I make it,' so I pretended to be just fine. As Mack growled, I spoke softly to him, tossing treats at him with every step. I even sang him a tune, though I will admit it was a bit out of key. I visited Mack for several days, offering food and Bruce Springsteen songs, but my affection was continually met with resistance.

One day I reached the rear enclosure and was surprised to find that Mack tolerated my touch. But when my leash went around his neck, it was more than he could stand. Mack became a bucking bronco, pulling hard, falling behind, and then refusing to budge. Walking Mack was torture — for both of us. Later I found out that Mack and his brother, Riley, who lived in the cage next to him, had spent most of their two years living in a car. They'd never been walked or socialized and were therefore fearful of people, loud noises and anything out of the usual. Since walking Mack and Riley was out, and cars were what they knew, my Volvo station wagon became their chariot, and the local dog park their haven.

Mack and Riley loved their outings, and the more they got out, the more their demeanors improved. Despite their progress, however, the shelter owner told me that these dogs would never get adopted and they needed their cages for other dogs who actually stood a chance of finding a home. When she said she was planning on euthanizing them, I officially became Mack and Riley's guardian and spent the next six months trying to find them their forever homes.

Finally, one splendid Sunday, a mom and her young daughter came to the shelter and fell in love with Riley, and despite his fears, they brought him home.

Mack's day finally came too. But his forever home would not be in Los Angeles, where we lived, but in Helena, Montana, a three-day car ride away.

Driving through freezing temperatures alone and with a fearful dog was not an idea I relished, but I knew this was Mack's only chance...

If you would like to know how Mack's story ends — and begins, pick up your copy of *Dog as My Doctor, Cat as My Nurse: An animal lover's guide to a healthy, happy & extraordinary life* online or from your favorite bookstore today!

"The Tao of Pooh meets *The Dog Whisperer.* A must read."

— Readers Favorite Book Review

Coming Soon...

Are you more of a cat & kitty lover? If so, keep an eye out for *Paws for the Good Stuff: A cat lover's journal for creating a happier & more pawsitive life.*

Share your stories, anecdotes, and pictures of you with your BFF at AnimalHumanHealth.com

89350067R00141

Made in the USA
San Bernardino, CA
23 September 2018